Surviving Inside The Kill Zone

The Essential Tools You Need to Survive Deadly Combat

Writings of Purpose and Intent

By

Ernest Emerson

Cover Photo by Kevin Falerios
kevinfaleriosphotography.com

Copyright ©2015 Ernest Emerson

All rights reserved. No part of this book may be reproduced, stored in a retrieval system, or transcribed, in any form or by any means, electronic, mechanical, photocopying, recording, or otherwise, without prior permission of the author.

ISBN-13: 978-1507785966

ISBN-10: 1507785968

About the author:

Ernest Emerson is the founder and owner of the company, Emerson Knives, Inc., and is considered, "The Father of Tactical Knives," having designed the most iconic and well known combat knives in history.

He is a Black Belt Hall of Fame member and United States Martial Arts Hall of Fame Member and is a "Tier One" hand-to-hand combat and edged weapons instructor who has taught his combat system to many of the world's most deadly warriors, including the U.S. Navy SEAL Teams, U.S. Marines, U.S. Army Special Forces and various Government agencies.

Sir Ernest Emerson is a Knight of The Noble Order of the Black Shamrock and also holds the coveted title of Master-at-Arms. He is a noted lecturer, author and is an expert witness for the Los Angeles District Attorney's Office in deadly force cases. He has appeared on many T.V. shows, radio programs and has acted as a technical expert on numerous award winning movies.

His background includes playing professional baseball, boxing, Jeet Kune Do and Gracie Jiu Jitsu. He is the founder of The Emerson Combat System and is the owner of the Black Shamrock Combat Academy in Los Angeles, California.

He is the husband of a beautiful wife and the father to three wonderful children. Mr. Emerson is a Rock n' Roll junkie and enjoys the taste of fine Scotch whiskey. He may be contacted at info@emersonknives.com.

Dedication

Dedicated to all those who know our fight has just begun and stand ready and willing to sacrifice everything to preserve our way of life. There is no higher calling.

Disclaimer

Please note that the author is NOT RESPSONSIBLE in any manner whatsoever for any injury that may result from practicing the techniques and/or following the instructions given within. Since the physical activities described herein may be too strenuous in nature for some readers to engage in safely, it is essential that a physician be consulted prior to training.

Emerson's Commandments of A Warrior

1. Protect the weak
2. Defend the innocent
3. Standup to tyranny and unjust behavior
4. Take responsibility for your actions and be prepared to accept the consequences
5. Honor friendship with loyalty
6. Stand tall in the face of adversity
7. Ask more of yourself than others
8. Never do anything without a purpose
9. Never do anything that is useless
10. Be honest in your intentions and actions with everyone you meet

Table of Contents

Introduction..9

Chapter 1. Education..........................13

Learning the tactics, strategies, motives, history, and weapon systems of the enemy.

Chapter 2. Training............................18

Hard skills learning process, shooting skills, hand-to-hand combat, and weapons.

Chapter 3. Conditioning....................60

Combat strength and physical fitness, combat endurance, and functional strength.

Chapter 4. Awareness........................65

Tactical awareness, situational awareness and the states of vigilance.

Chapter 5. Mindset............................74

The warrior mindset, self-motivation, never quit and never give up.

Chapter 6. Goals..................................79

Setting goals: Extreme goals and extreme efforts equals extreme results. Do your behaviors support your goals?

Chapter 7. Capacity..........................83

Capability needs capacity. The willingness to execute with violence of action.

Conclusion......................................90

Introduction

All Fighting is Fighting

As long as man has walked upon this earth, man has fought upon this earth. As my friend Ken, a wrestling coach once told me, track and field was invented when the first two cavemen ran chasing after a deer and the fastest caveman caught it. Wrestling was invented when the second cave man caught up.

Much has changed over the millennia since the time of those cavemen. First we threw rocks and sticks, then we went on to make tools which doubled as weapons, by striking two pieces of stone together called flint knapping. It wasn't long until someone found out that by tying a cord to both ends of a springy piece of wood he could shoot a sharpened stick faster and farther than he could throw it. Someone also figured out how to mine copper which was harder than wood and easier to work than stone and then, when combined with tin copper became bronze, a metal hard enough for daggers, swords, and spears. Bronze begat iron. Iron begat steel, an even harder metal, suitable for arms, armament, and armor. Then along came gunpowder and man's weapons could reach out farther and create much more destruction than ever before. This constant progression continued on and on without cessation giving us tanks, airplanes, warships and ICBMs with nuclear warheads.

But although the means of fighting over the ownership of that deer for dinner has evolved and mutated tens of thousands of times, there is one weapons system that has not evolved. In fact it has not changed once since man became man. That thing that has never changed is man, and he is defined by the same primal principles as those first two cavemen wrestling over that deer. The primal principles are those which define the essence, the core of human conflict, man-to-man, hand-to-hand, life-and-death combat. As much as all the thousands of years of evolution has changed the means by which combat between opponents is fought, there is still a man, a human being behind each weapon, pulling the trigger or pushing the button. Man is still the universal common denominator in all combat. And, more to the point, no matter what the evolutionary sophistication of weapons and their means of delivery become, there is and always will be the need, the requirement, or necessity of the individual human being to go into harm's way. Men will still be called to face the rigors, the danger, the reality, and the finality, of man-to-man combat. Whether it be facing an armed intruder in your home, an active shooter in a robbery, or a terrorist hiding in the next room, the need for an individual civilian, a police officer or a soldier to be willing and able to fight "tooth and nail," against an evil entity, cloaked in the guise of a fellow human will remain with us as long as man continues to walk on this planet.

I must remind you that this book is based upon the premise that you are facing or imminently about to face a deadly attack--an attacker who has left you no other option than to either kill or be killed. I will for the sake of the reader state that all your other options have already been exhausted. There is no way left to avoid it. There's no chance to escape. There is no chance to de-escalate and there is no other choice except to fight for your very survival. Keep this in mind as you read further. The title is, after all, "Surviving Inside the Kill Zone."

Chapter 1.

Education

Knowledge destroys fear. It is human nature that we fear what we do not know. I believe it is one of the most basic survival skills that we are born with. It is natural that we all become victims of it to some degree at various times in our lives. Such fear is an obstacle, a big one. Fear makes us hesitate. Fear makes us question our abilities. It shakes our confidence. Fear dulls our edge and saps our strength. Fear gives our enemies their power. We fear what we think is dangerous, or what could cause us harm, or what we think is more powerful than us. And never forget this, "power perceived is power achieved."

There is an antidote, a cure for fear and it is simple. That cure, that antidote, is knowledge. To gain that knowledge you must seek it. You must spend time and effort to gain it. Because it requires a little extra effort, a little work, and some honest self-evaluation, it is the reason why so many have never conquered their own simple personal fears. It's just easier to live with the hope that you will never have to face your fear than it is to face it and conquer it. The simple truth is that the more we know about something, the less we fear it. Fear I believe, is an irrational emotion. Now don't misunderstand what I'm stating, conquering fear with knowledge does not negate or take away danger. Danger is real. Danger hurts. Danger kills. Fear does not. But if you are embraced by the irrational fear of something that is truly dangerous, you cannot formulate a *rational* plan to combat or negate that danger. In a perfect world, you would be aware of danger, you would respect it, and you would acknowledge it as a potential threat, but you would not fear it. Of course things always sound easier than they really are and this is definitely not a perfect world.

In terms of a threat to personal safety (in this case a deadly attack) in order to come up with a working plan or solution to combat such extreme physical violence, you must apply the same formula. You must educate yourself about the enemy or potential enemies. You need to learn their tactics and strategies, their most likely moves, their modus operandi. I also believe in addition to that, you must also become aware of their motivations, their convictions, their history and of course their weapon systems. In understandable terms, you would deal much differently with the mugger who just wants your wallet so he can buy his next meth high than you would with the suicide jihadist who not only wants to kill as many innocents as he can, but also himself, in the process.

Most criminal acts and also terrorist acts, follow a pattern. Even if it is only a general pattern, there is still a pattern in there somewhere. Here are some examples: it is almost always the case that if a mugger, a rapist or an attacker binds you, ties you up, or attempts to remove you from the scene of the initial attack, his plan is to kill you. It is also true that in any hostage takeover situation, the best time to escape is in the chaos and confusion at the beginning of the attack, because the bad guy's next move is to round everyone up to control the situation and the hostages, rendering the chance of escape virtually impossible.

It is also true that almost all attacks are in the form of an ambush and involve the element of surprise or a distraction to be successful. For example, I've always taught my wife and my daughters to never park next to a van and to always park where it's well lit. By the way, using a van is the same tactic we (the good guys) use to do a snatch and grab, because it works so well. Although I'm using these simple common sense anecdotes as examples to make a point, there are hundreds if not thousands who fall prey to predators every year because they are not aware of these three simple bits of knowledge.

I am an eternal student. I am a student of human nature, of human interaction, of human conflict, and of human reaction to conflict. I'm a student of criminal behavior, criminal gangs, of terrorists and the acts of terrorism. I pay attention not only to trends in criminal behavior but also to the cluster effects of terrorist or criminal acts. In terms of becoming aware of criminal trends one sometimes only needs to watch the evening news. For example, a serious criminal trend called the knockout game has recently gone viral among young street punks in cities across the US. For those of you who do not know what it is, I will educate you. As an unsuspecting victim passes by a group of three or more punks "minding his own business" one of them steps out and cold cocks the unaware victim with a sucker punch that knocks the person out cold. The victim could be anyone, 12 years old to 85 years old, male or female. I've seen film of an 85-year-old grandmother that after being struck, she hit the deck so hard that her head bounced off the ground. I believe she ended up in a coma. I've seen a 40-year-old man in a business suit carrying a briefcase hit so hard that he fell face first against the curb, dying from the impact--all for the laughs and giggles of some stupid ass punks playing a *game*. Do you think I pay a little more attention now when I'm out walking and need to pass some teenagers loitering, and hanging out, on the sidewalk? You only get one guess to answer that question.

People often ask me, why do you always want to face the door or sit next to an exit in a restaurant, theater or at any public event? Well, the simple answer, the only answer, is so I can see who is coming into the establishment and if shit hits the fan, I can get my family out of danger fast.

In the event of an attack or terrorist event, such as the Nairobi mall attack, things happen in milliseconds that can spell the difference between being a casualty and being home that night with your family. Educating yourself about the actions of potential attackers and then being able to plot solutions to their actions is actually the easiest of the seven essential skills to acquire yet is probably the most overlooked and neglected of all. After all, you can acquire this skill in the safety and comfort of your own home with just a few good informative books. In fact, I'll give you a good list of recommended reading at the end of this book.

Chapter 2.

Training

If you think something is necessary, do it every day. If it's not necessary, don't do it at all. **– Dan Gable**

As important as training is, it's only half of the physical side of preparation. The other half we will discuss in the next chapter. This half will deal with what I call the *hard skills,* the techniques, and the mechanical skills needed to prepare for combat. These hard skills include shooting classes, self-defense courses, and martial arts training.

In regard to shooting classes, it could be handgun, rifle or shotgun classes which would teach the use and function of the weapon as well as all of the safety protocols associated with that specific weapon system being taught. If you are a novice, you will need to purchase a gun or guns to have for self-defense. You may choose to have a pistol, a rifle, a shotgun or better yet, all three in your arsenal. You may decide to own only a pistol or any combination of the three choices, but I would say this in regard to choices, always buy a pistol. If you don't get a pistol, buy a shotgun. A shotgun is a pretty good all round defensive weapon if you could only own one gun. The rifle, for most who are primarily interested in home defense, is the last choice. A pistol is my first choice for use in my house. It is more maneuverable and it holds more rounds than a shotgun. However, I'll tell you this, having lived through the LA riots, I sat on top of my house with a 12 gauge shotgun to ward off the rioters that came to our neighborhood. Seeing my shotgun probably saved my house, seeing me with only a pistol may not have done so. Everyone knows a shotgun will blow a hole big enough to drive a truck through. At least that's what *they* think and that works in our favor. But, by this example you can also see that sometimes you might need to take your gun fight outside of your home where more distance to the target becomes a factor which weighs against a pistol as a primary weapon or a visual deterrent.

At the same time, I 100% recommend that you get your concealed carry weapons permit for your state, county or city, whatever the case may be. In this case I'm definitely talking about a pistol. Let's just look at this in regard to carrying a pistol outside of your home. What if you are at a mall and some bad guy pulls out a weapon and starts killing women, children, and innocent bystanders. You need to know that in almost every single case of schools, malls, or theater shootings, it took a gun to stop the gun.

The pistol is a gun that you would always have with you; a rifle or shotgun you would not.

In regard to buying a rifle, I will offer this; if you cannot obtain or afford a new pistol or shotgun, you can always purchase rifles as surplus or used, at discount prices. There are many good choices for the surplus rifles out there and many of them can be purchased and taken home with you right out of the shop. And as long as you have ammo for it, any gun is still better than no gun. Sitting on top of my roof with a rifle would still have probably been as good a visual deterrent to those rioters as my shotgun was. Speaking to those of you who may not yet own a firearm, since there are hundreds of brands, models, and calibers to choose from, I'll give you my recommendations to help you with your choices.

In choosing a pistol, I recommend a Glock. Specifically either the Glock 19, or the Glock 17, both of which are 9 mm caliber. Here's my short list of reasons why:

1. They are readily available.

2. They run forever and are one of the most dependable pistols of all times.

3. You can buy a used one and it will still run forever.

4. 9 mm ammo is readily available.

5. The Glock 19 (compact) holds 15 rounds in the magazine. The Glock 17 (full size) holds 17 rounds in the magazine. **Please Note;** check your local and state laws for maximum magazine capacity allowed. Some states allow only 10 round magazines.

6. They are easier and quicker to get back on target after each round is fired.

Contrary to all of the arguments about bullet caliber, stopping power, and the *bigger is better* arguments, statistics have shown that it is the number of rounds delivered to the target that stops an attack *regardless* of caliber size. Please do not engage me in any arguments about the size of the bullet. I am not saying that I don't know about delivered kinetic energy, wound channels and ballistic capabilities. I do. I also know that a 9 mm does not flip or kick nearly as much as a larger caliber round such as 45 ACP. Therefore it is easier for the *average* shooter to re-acquire the target after each trigger press. Which, if you have had the proper training will give you the opportunity to deliver more rounds into the intended target, more quickly.

My recommendation for a shotgun is the Remington 870, 12 gauge. They're like a Chevy truck. They've been around forever, there are a million parts and accessories available for them, and there are plenty of used ones available on the market. Twelve-gauge is the caliber of the 870 and is always the best choice, even if you don't get a Remington. The reason is that you can get a variety of loads, (different sized pellets in the shotgun shell), including buckshot and slugs if you choose. They pack a hell of a wallop into a target and since they spread their bullets out after leaving the barrel of the weapon one does not have to be as precise in aiming as with a pistol or a rifle. And I will also add this; every bad guy in the world knows the sound of a round being racked into the chamber of a pump action 12 gauge shotgun. They also know what sound will be next.

When it comes to owning a rifle, I will recommend any AR-15 platform or style (the black gun, assault rifle) in 5.56 caliber. But you will still have to make a choice. There are simply too many brands out there to pick one over another. I'll leave that choice up to you depending on how much you want to spend. The AR – 15 platform is one of the firearms industries' greatest innovations in that it is made up of a number of user friendly parts and it is so boneheaded simple to disassemble and reassemble that there are now more companies making parts for that rifle than there are companies making the rifle itself and there are plenty of companies making the rifle. You can customize, fit and build the AR-15 to suit your body size, your environment, and any other requirements you might have. It is a battle proven weapons platform that has been carried by U.S. soldiers for decades. The only caveat is this. If you think you want one of these rifles, I'd get one because the way things are going, sooner or later, they are going to ban them for whatever silly reason they can concoct. I suppose, and I fear that the same advice also goes for pistols and shotguns.

So now that we've talked about the types and caliber of firearms I believe you should own, let's take a short look at firearms training. Your firearms training should consist of a *minimum* of a two-day course in the safe handling of your firearm, range safety, and basic marksmanship skills. This should be classified as an introductory level class and should acquaint you with proper sight alignment, proper grip and stance, weapons presentation, loading and unloading the weapon, along with the awareness of how to clear most common malfunctions. Whether your class teaches it or not, you must also commit not only to memory, but into practice, the following rules of gun safety and awareness.

1. All guns are always loaded, always.

2. Never point your gun at anything you do not want to destroy.

3. Keep your finger off the trigger until your sights are on the target.

4. Identify your target and what is behind it. Never shoot at anything unless you have positively identified the target.

If your firearms class does not advocate and adhere to at least a variation of these four basic rules, find another shooting school quickly.

You must possess a competency at a level equal to or better than having completed the basic marksmanship training for any of your weapons before you can safely and confidently progress to the next level, *tactical training*.

Bear in mind, a four hour range seminar isn't going to do it. *Uncle Bob taught me how to shoot,* isn't going to do it. A husband is not a good teacher either. True professional instructors follow a curriculum, have experience and expertise in this field and have generally taught hundreds of students before teaching you. Professional instructors know what they're doing and if they are a professional, they will cover everything you're supposed to cover in an introductory class and they will make sure you've got it, including basic legal precautions concerning the use of a firearm. By the way, a class with 100 students doesn't cut it. A class size of up to 25 students max with at least two auxiliary instructors or safety officers, is minimally acceptable.

Realistic tactical training is where things start to come together, and you will soon see how easy it was when you were just standing on the firing range shooting at fixed paper targets. Tactical instruction will include areas of instruction in the tactics strategies and practice of using your gun in a real gunfight, or at least as close as they can get to one in a teaching situation. These areas will cover things like, engaging multiple targets, moving targets, shooting from cover and other physical positions. They should include advanced malfunction drills, tactical reloads and the introduction of stress while performing all of the above. If you go on to advanced training, Simunitions training is some of the best and most realistic training available. Simunitions training involves shooting wax pellets from actual cartridges with only a primer charge in the round, using modified versions of your actual carry gun. It allows you to engage in very realistic gunfights with opponents who are actually firing back at you and you can run an infinite number of scenarios to gain first-hand experience. When you get hit by a simmunition round, they hurt like hell and they are about as close to the real thing as you can get. Noise, pain and adrenaline make for a serious learning curve. It is a serious reality check for what you can actually do versus what you think you can do under stress. It's the place for you to make mistakes and work through them in practice so you don't make them when it's for real. Now I must caution you to do your school work before you choose your shooting instruction or school. It's one of the most important investments you'll ever make. Treat it as such. Let me put it like this. If I had $1000 to spend and the best shooting school cost $900, I'd buy a $100 gun.

In speaking to those of you who might be reluctant to own a firearm for self-defense, I'll thank God if I never have to pull my gun out of my holster, but I will also thank God I have a gun, when I have no choice but to use it.

There are two fighting skills that you must learn and practice in order to prepare yourself to meet the force of a deadly attack. These two fighting skills are categorized as *armed* and *unarmed*. The category of *armed* combat skills are further divided into two groups; *hot weapons*, (firearms) and *cold weapons*, any other hand-held weapon such as a knife, club, or striking weapon, etc. Since I have already talked about the aspect of hot weapons training (firearms) we will now move on to the other half of combat.

It seems popular these days to also divide unarmed combat in into two categories, stand up fighting and ground fighting. However, I have strong opinions in this regard. In my view and experience, a fight is a fight whether you are standing up or rolling around on the ground. You better be able to fight either way. In regard to searching for an instructor or school, I will warn you of that if an instructor tells you that all you need to know is standup fighting and that he has all the answers, then he doesn't know how to grapple. If an instructor tells you that all you need to know is grappling, then he doesn't know how to box. The simple truth is that you need both. Today there are plenty of schools that teach both stand up and grappling. Any MMA gym would be a good start. Watch out for Tae Kwon Do. It will get you smoked in a real fight. My personal background is in high school wrestling, Jeet Kune Do, Filipino Kali, amateur boxing, and Gracie Jiujitsu, all full contact fighting systems where all training was against spontaneous opponents who were trying to hurt me as much as I was trying to hurt them. In order to be effective, any school must spend time on spontaneous full contact sparring, whether it's with headgear and gloves or in a gi rolling around on the ground.

The hardest thing to teach novice boxers to do is to learn how to *get hit,* simply because it's not in our best interest to get hit by anything, and we have instinctively learned how to avoid it. Until the novice boxer learns to stand his ground and fire back while taking a few punches, he'll spend all of his time trying to stay out of range and avoid getting hit or even touched for that matter. The problem is that by staying out of the opponent's range, he's also out of your range. You can't hit him if he can't hit you. Unfortunately in a fight, you're going to get hit and if you fall apart like a *cheap suit* the first time you get clobbered, you'll probably end up in the morgue. The goal of *full contact* training is that you'll never know how much you can take unless you take it. And you'll be surprised at how much you *can* take. The key is that you don't want to get hit hard for the first time in a real fight. You'll hear more about that later. Remember this: the longer the fight goes on, the greater the chance of a lucky and maybe a *deadly* shot getting to its target. Contrary though it may seem, the same rules apply to edged weapons and impact weapons as well. You have to be in range to fight, strike, or damage the opponent. If you are out of range, then there is no fight in which case you should *stay* out of range, if that is a viable option. The *fight dancing* that most martial arts teach, where you dance back and forth with your opponent will either get you beat like an old rug or sliced up like a Cobb salad. That's because most martial arts are taught by instructors who are far removed from the harsh realities of life and death combat. Here are two golden rules about hand-to-hand combat training:

1. Everything you are taught should be a perfect technique.

Okay, what do I mean, *perfect technique?* Well the definition of a perfect technique is this:

A. It gives you a tactical advantage.

B. It negates or worsens the tactical advantage of the threat.

C. It protects you from harm.

D. It damages, unbalances or destroys the threat.

If any technique you have been taught is not supported by those strategies, don't waste your time. Remember, this is about life or death. Do you recall the quote by Dan Gable at the beginning of this chapter? "If you think something is necessary do it every day. If it's not necessary don't do it at all." I will also add what I stress over and over again in my classes, "Never do anything that is useless. Never do anything without a purpose." When your life or the life of your loved ones, or teammates, is on the line, everything you do *must* abide by those rules.

2. Everything you are taught should be *with bad intent*.

Now what do I mean by this statement **with bad intent?** Well, first I'm going to ask this question. Why do some people hit so much harder than others? Let's take a look at the five components of hitting with ultimate power. In order to hit as hard as you possibly can, the following attributes have to be present in the process;

A. Timing – you have to hit where he's at.

B. Accuracy – you need to hit what will hurt.

C. Speed – it's about Newtonian physics – mass x acceleration = power.

D. Perfect body mechanics – all your power must be channeled into the punch.

E. Proper mental attitude – the X factor – *Bad Intent*.

Mike Tyson in his prime was quite probably the hardest punching heavyweight boxer of all times. When interviewed after a string of 12 knockouts, many of them in under a minute of the first round, a reporter asked, "How can you knock people out with a body shot, without even hitting them in the head?" Mike replied simply, "You have to throw your punches *with bad intent.*"

So, if you look at the five attributes necessary for ultimate punching power and the explanation of one of the hardest hitters of all times, you'll notice that they both include *attitude* as one of the necessary attributes needed to generate ultimate power. The fact is that it doesn't just apply to punching. It applies to punches, kicks, throws, arm bars, locks, rips, tears and head butts also. Bad intent is just as necessary for every one of those techniques to be the most effective as it is for Mike Tyson's punches. In terms of recommending various martial arts, Krav Maga is certainly one that fills the bill for *real* combat effectiveness. What is the reason? After all, they use the same punches and kicks as all the other martial arts. Well, the simple truth is that what separates Krav Maga from other physically similar martial arts, the main difference, is the attitude and intent. Everything is done with *violence of action.* Everything is done with the intent and intensity needed to maim, incapacitate or kill the opponent. Believe me, the Israelis have plenty of experience in fighting to kill or be killed and it shows in their martial art, Krav Maga. Everything they do is done *with bad intent.*

Attitude can make all the difference. Attitude can spell the difference between life and death. So if your hand-to-hand combat training is not built on the foundation I've previously described of spontaneity, full contact, the perfect technique, and bad intent, then you need to find one that is. Which again brings us back to the original quote by Dan Gable at the beginning of this chapter: "If it's important do it every day. If it's not don't do it at all."

Note; Dan Gable, Olympic gold medalist is one of the greatest wrestlers of all time and considered one of the greatest coaches of all times. His high school record was 64 – 0, with 3 state titles. His college record was 117 – 1 with 2 national titles. He was an Olympic gold medalist in the Munich games in 1972. As a coach, Dan Gable won 15 NCAA wrestling championships while compiling a record of 355 – 21 – 5. He coached 152 All Americans, 45 national champions, 106 Big Ten champions and 12 Olympians including 4 gold medalists.

In order to train in the use of *cold weapons*, knives or impact weapons, (the ones that don't go bang), all of the above also applies. Fighting is fighting, combat is combat. It doesn't matter what weapon you have in your hand, knife, gun, or clenched fist. When I teach an edged weapons program, there is a primary goal or objective that I always have in mind. I need to turn each trainee into a fighter first before I ever let them pick up a knife. That way I've always got a fighter in front of me and then it doesn't matter what weapon they've got in their hand. If I started them with knives right away then I would just have a bunch of weak fighters with knives in their hands dependent upon their weapon to make them a fighter. The weapon does not make the fighter. The man makes the fighter. Fortunately for me, I was taught something very important by a very dangerous man, many years ago. He told me, "Ernest, you have far more to fear from a deadly man than from a deadly weapon." He knew exactly what he was talking about.

Let me talk a little bit about edged weapons and the current state of training.

Less is More

Edged weapons training is rife with so called experts teaching techniques and methods that they themselves could never pull off in a real fight even with their decades of experience and daily training routines. Sure they look impressive in front of a class with their assistants or a compliant student, but I'm talking about an edged weapon here, a deadly weapon. One that is only called to use if someone is trying to kill you. In this case you are going to need to do what works - not what looks impressive. That is the difference, the whole difference-- the difference between life and death.

People have grown used to the idea that more is better and that the more complex something is, the better it is. And so it is with edged weapons training. What's wrong is that this mentality does not apply to fighting and especially not in a life or death situation when someone is truly bent on doing you harm.

Let me give you an example. Recently I taught an advanced edged weapons class to a mix of Military and Police Officers. There were several students there from a local martial arts school in attendance with dozens of years of training experience in an Eastern edged weapons system that included a myriad of disarming techniques. Little did they know that I had over a decade of experience in the same system. Anyway, at lunch break on the second day, one of them expressed a concern that what I was teaching was not *advanced edged weapons* because I didn't include knife disarms and takeaways.

"Well after 12 years of study you must know some disarms," I said.

"I know quite a few," was his reply.

"Can you disarm me?" I asked.

"I believe I can" he replied. And so we squared off. Holding the knife in my right hand, I struck toward his face with a jab. His hands went up to block just as I was shooting in for his legs (the jab was long gone before he even raised his hands). I took him down immediately, mounted, and had my knife across his neck.

"You were going to fight me with a knife," he said.

I replied. "I didn't fight you. I killed you. You want to try again?"

"Yes!" Once again we squared off. This time I merely held the knife behind my back. From a left lead, I threw a left jab as I jammed forward, the knife still behind my back. He raised his hands and tried to block the jab (obviously not a boxer) and we ended up chest to chest. I circled my knife hand around his back, trapped his right arm with my left, stepped in front of him and executed a classic hip throw, dragging my knife across his throat as he went down. I stabbed him twice under the arm and once in the neck just as he hit the mat.

"You can't hide the knife. How can I disarm you if you're hiding it?" he asked as he was standing up, (not in base by the way). And now I couldn't resist.

"Son, you never learned the first rule of knife fighting. There ain't no rules."

At this point he was more than a little pissed off. Not even asking if he wanted to go again, I gave him the knife and said, "Now let's see what happens." He dropped into a classic knife fighter's stance. *Whatever that is.* He lunged at me with a #1 and #2 strike pattern. I think it caught him off guard that I didn't back up but framed against my head (the boxer defense against the hook) and charged forward. When I hit him, I wrapped my left arm over his right (knife arm) and executed another hip throw. I kept his knife arm trapped and dropped my knee to the side of his head pinning him to the ground. I pinned his knife arm at the elbow across my thighs. I said, "Drop your knife." He was pretty pissed and resisted. I said, "Drop the knife or I'll break your arm." I pressed harder against my thigh. He wouldn't let go. I said, "I'm not being nice anymore, I'm going to slam your arm across my thigh and it *will* fuck your elbow up. Drop it now!"

And he let go. I stood over him. "That is a disarm. The kind that actually works and this is what I teach in my class. You can call it advanced or not. I don't give a shit."

"All I know, is that with your twelve years of experience, you couldn't execute a disarm. You couldn't counter a basic double leg takedown. You couldn't stop an attack. You couldn't keep me from killing you. Maybe you should go back to your 'advanced training' for another 12 years. I don't train to fight - I fight. Get out of my class. I'll refund your money." He grabbed his gear and left.

Put on some head gear, a mouth guard, a groin protector and go full speed, at full contact. You'll find out right away what works and what doesn't. And you'll also learn that there is no knife fighting. It's fighting...with a knife. That's the difference. You may think my actions in this case harsh or even arrogant. But you need to understand this: I don't do this for fun or sport or some deep philosophical revelation, and I've not spent a huge part of my life getting my ass kicked by someone else because it's a hobby, It's my way of life and I don't take disrespect lightly. You see, I'm all about fighting and I've been in enough of them to know what is real and what is theory. If I can't do what I teach, I don't teach it. If I can teach something the average man can't do, I don't teach it. If an average-sized man can't do what I teach, I don't teach it. It really is that simple.

This whole event reminds me of another seminar I was teaching several years ago when a well-known knife maker who made tactical and fighting knives *based on his experience* (3rd degree black belt in his bio), showed up at the class. When I noticed him there (he was talking rather loudly while I was teaching), I walked over and invited him into the class.

"I'll comp you in," I told him. He was more than a little on the spot.

"No man, I hurt my back the other day training."

"Really," I said. "I've got a torn rotator, a slipped disc and a knee that pops out a couple times a day."

"Sorry you've got a sore back, maybe some other time. I'd love to get you on the mat." He got up and left. Sorry about the long rant. I'm just so tired of bullshit.

Think about it like this. Have you ever seen a boxer so fast and accurate that he could just pick off the other guys punches as fast as the opponent could throw them? I'll answer that question for you. **No**, you haven't, and no, you never will. The reason is that one human cannot react faster than the other human can act. That is why boxing is so much more effective than classical Karate. Karate still thinks it can block punches. You'd think after 500 years or so they would've learned *something*.

Boxing knows better. In boxing the defense is set up to put obstacles or *roadblocks* in the way to protect the target, generally your head, and the opponent has to punch through them in order to strike the target. Since boxing is real fighting, boxing knows you cannot react fast enough to stop a spontaneous punch once it starts. You may anticipate a punch and get lucky once in a while, but you cannot beat a punch when it starts first. That's why you keep your hands up and close to your head in boxing, so you have something in the way if and when those punches are thrown.

Which brings us back to knives. Most schools and systems teach a complex series of blocks, parries and very cool disarms. Now I'll ask another question. If you can't do it in boxing, why do you think you can do it against a knife? Well, the simple answer is that you still can't react faster than someone else can act. Now, I'm the first to tell you that I'm no Bruce Lee, but I can tell you that in over 40 years of training, teaching, and fighting, I've never had anyone execute a knife disarm on me unless I let them, and even then, a highly skilled practitioner couldn't do it if I moved more than around half speed. Like I say in class, it's like trying to hit a mosquito with a dart. So if you can't do it in a training, let alone a real fight, is it important? If something is important do it every day, if it's not important don't do it at all.

Unfortunately so much of what is being taught about edged weapons is not only not important, it is useless, but I guess in the end, it's still deadly... for you.

As I've stated earlier, the universal principles of combat do not care who they apply to, whether you are good or bad, whether you are skilled or unskilled. They are in play all the time. They never sleep and they never stop. So if the universal rules apply at all times in human conflict and apply to all fighting and all types fighting, it doesn't matter if you're fighting with your bare hands, with a knife, a stick, a club, or a rock.

On Combat

I would like you to read something. It's a set of four simple rules of combat.

1. Attack First – Seize the initiative by attacking the enemy before he can attack you. This attack should be relentless until the enemy is struck down, for he cannot attack you if he is preoccupied with his own defense.

2. Defend Yourself by Counterattacking – If you need to protect yourself from an attack by your opponent, use a technique that also counterattacks.

3. Stay Near the Opponent's Weapon – Should you bind against your opponent's weapon, or lay hands upon him to grapple, you should try to work in such a way that you are never far from his weapon or person so that you can control and limit his actions.

4. Use Strength Against Weakness and Weakness Against Strength – If your opponent weakly resists your offense, then overpower him and complete the attack. If he opposes you strongly, yield to his strength and attack from a different side or angle instead. Never use strength against strength, for this puts victory in the hands of brute strength, not skill.

These are the words **written over 700 years ago,** of Johannes Lichtenauer – Father of German Swordsmanship in the 14th Century.

Johannes Lichtenauer, one of the greatest knightly fighting instructors of all times, also leaves us with the following quote, "All fighting is fighting."

These words were true in a time when the only combat there was, was man-to-man combat and they are truly relevant today. After all we still only have two arms and two legs. Nothing in that regard has changed.

In terms of edged weapons, a fight is still a fight and if you are learning or being taught some complex technical skills that someone has said will work in combat, well quite frankly, and very honestly, they won't. They're fun and they are impressive, but they're just fun and impressive. They are not combat skills. It has been told to me that the best knife fighting technique is a good right cross. I won't argue that. In fact one of the statements that I make in my classes is this "If you want to be a knife fighter, learn how to box." Every skill you need to wield an edged weapon effectively is contained in boxing. If you put a knife in the hand of a good boxer you've already got a pretty good knife fighter. There is an analogy with a real good example of what I'm describing. I trained for many years at the top training facility in the world, the first and foremost full contact fighting school taught by two of the most famous and revered fighting instructors in the history of the martial arts. They introduced full contact martial arts training and edged weapons training to America and literally the rest the world. At that school, we learned, in addition to boxing and unarmed hand-to-hand combat, the use of just about every weapon you can pick up and hold in your hands. We spent hours learning and practicing stick fighting skills and every dis-arm, dislocate, strike, poke, flail and pattern combination that exists. They were intricate, complex and a hell of a lot of fun. But every Thursday night was full contact stick fighting night, where we would square off against an opponent and fight three two-minute rounds at full speed, full contact. We wore eye protection, boxing headgear, a cup and the precursors to MMA gloves. And I'll tell you this, there were broken and dislocated fingers, hematomas on the ears and numerous contusions and bone bruises as a result. But I noticed that there were no disarms, dislocates, or locks, like we all practiced in class. The only disarms were when someone was struck so hard in the hand that they dropped their stick. In fact what I saw, what I experienced, was two combatants trying to hit each other as hard as humanly possible. Eventually I talked to the instructor and told him, "I know we practice all this other stuff, but I only see two guys trying to hit each other as hard as possible when they are actually fighting. Shouldn't I just be practicing learning how to hit as hard as humanly possible?" "Ernest," he replied, "You have just reached a level of understanding that few of these students will ever attain. The essence of combat is not only being able to know what works but also in being able to discern what will not work. How many students do you think we could keep, if every day they would come in and spend two hours swinging their sticks at a heavy bag? We have to teach all the other stuff so they think they're getting their money's worth and that there is still more to learn. That is the "art" of combat but not the combat of combat. Go and practice learning how to hit as hard as humanly possible. That is combat and not art." I followed his advice. Bruce Lee once said, "I do not fear the man who has practiced a thousand kicks. I fear the man who has practiced one kick 1000 times."

The legionary soldiers of the Roman armies, one of the most effective and feared fighting forces in history were required to spend one hour a day striking a wooden pole with a wooden sword. Once again we find another universal truth proven in combat that cannot be ignored. If it was good enough for a Roman soldier, who fought hand-to-hand in every battle they engaged, then it is good enough for me.

I hope that you now realize that everything I have said so far in this book also applies to edged weapons and knives. This is not a book of techniques and although I may discuss a technique for the purpose of illustrating a point, it is a book of principles, a book of attributes that are the *true secrets* to effectiveness in real life or death combat. I cannot teach you knife fighting techniques in a book, just as I cannot teach you how to swim or play the piano in a book. What I'm trying to do is give you the insight and the ability to look at your own training program and to be able to start on the path to discarding what is not useful and keeping only what you need. It is important to develop the ability to divorce yourself completely from your experience, loyalty to your school and your instructor and place yourself objectively in the context where you would be facing a serious, violent and aggressive opponent attacking you with the intent of killing you. This changes everything. If what you are learning and practicing gives you any difficulty in perfectly executing what you are training, every time you try it against a friendly, training partner, why would you ever try doing that same thing against an opponent who is trying with all his might to take your life? In this case you don't get to try again, you get to die.

Now after all of this dissertation, just what are the universal rules and principles of combat? Remember that they are always in play and they apply equally as well to you as they do to your opponent. But by being aware of them you can and must manipulate and control them to your advantage in order to prevail and survive.

Three Rules to Live By

The principles and concepts necessary to survive the deadly attack

There are three fundamental rules to surviving a violent (deadly attack). These three rules are universal truths and they apply to all forms of combat; law enforcement confrontations, man to man, hand-to-hand combat, unit-to-unit combat as well as large scale military theater and warfare strategy.

They are,

1. Control of Distance

2. Making the opponent react to you, not you to him.

3. Destruction (incapacitating) of the opponent

Violate one of these principles and you may survive. Violate more than one of these rules and you lose every time.

One of the most fundamental principles of all combat is simply stated: *Techniques without strategy are useless.*

How does this concept, along with the three rules of combat apply to you and your training in regard to fighting and self-defense?

They are the very foundation around which all of your training should be built and what you should strive to accomplish in every physical confrontation that you encounter.

How do these strategies apply to surviving a deadly attack and how do we employ them?

1. Control of Distance, How can I control the distance between myself and the opponent?

A. Disengage, escape or avoid coming into the effective range of the opponent, stay out of range, or run away.

B. Take the distance away. If you can't get away, take it away. Close the distance, effectively getting inside the opponent's range. Think about how the clinch in boxing stops the punching effectiveness of the fighter being clinched.

Remember this: You must control the distance. He who controls distance controls the fight.

2. The opponent must react to you, not you to him.

A. Introduce movement, duck, take cover, or counterattack. He can't react faster than I can act. Staying put gets you killed. Moving keeps you alive.

B. Reverse the opponent's 100% mindset. Go from reactive defense to active offense as quickly as possible. The best defense against an ambush is to counterattack with overwhelming firepower. Just ask a U.S. Marine.

3. Destruction (incapacitating) of the opponent.

Five strategies to disable the opponent.

1. Destruction of balance

2. Obstruction of airways or blood flow

3. Obstruction of vision

4. Structural damage

5. Disruption of the nervous system

Here are the Principles of Combat, distilled down to its essential elements unchanged since man first discovered that he could walk on two feet, long, long ago.

INSTINCTUAL TRIGGERS

In any situation whether it is in the safety of home watching TV or in the heat of a firefight, we all respond to instinctual triggers. I am not referring to the fight or flight mechanism that is initiated under threat of danger, but something even more basic.

The instinctual triggers do not need danger to be initiated. Just as touching a hot stove produces a reflex reaction whether you are in danger or not, these instinctual or reflexive reactions happen any time they are triggered.

In terms of Defensive Tactics, or hand-to-hand combat, knowing how you are going to react when triggered and conversely, how to trigger these reactions in an opponent, allows you to use them to your advantage.

First, I want to state that the premise of this section is to discuss events that are taking place just prior to and during an attack, not the events leading up to the attack. These are things that are going on during the fight. How you stay out of it or prevent the fight, is another subject altogether.

THE STARTLE RESPONSE

This response is universal throughout nature and is common to almost all bipedal animals and to most 4-legged animals that spend time upright on their hind legs. This is actually a very complex mechanism and could be the subject of a book by itself. It is the core premise around which the Emerson Combat System is largely based and here is a brief description of the reaction.

Any time the true startle response is triggered, the human body reacts as follows:

1. The legs flex and the knees bend slightly to "spring load" a stance for immediate movement.

2. The stomach muscles tighten and contract to protect the midsection.

3. The shoulders contract inward and hunch up like you're doing a shrug—to protect the neck and frontal midline.

4. The hands and arms come up in front and the elbows contract inward. The fingers splay and extend and finish

in a position about mid-face level to also protect the eyes and neck area.

This response actually provides a natural fighting stance and gives the human being a good base from which to launch an attack, a strike, or a defense counter against an attack.

In order to use, enhance, and train this *startle reflex* to your advantage, start by doing the following: As you are the one who is usually not initiating the attack, you should practice going from a relaxed stance, jumping into or *"startling"* into the stance that I have just described. In our training courses we call it the "Universal Fighting Stance." Familiarize yourself with this spring--loaded stance and practice immediately launching a kick, punch, or strike out of this stance as you become more and more familiar with the natural balance and power that it provides. Do not be overly concerned with where your feet are—you'll know if you're balanced and it doesn't matter whether or not your right or left foot is forward. In a spontaneous attack you may be in the middle of a step and have no control over "right lead or left lead." I am aware that if you carry a gun, you must always try to protect your gun side, but in the case of a real blind side attack, you don't get to choose—at least at first.

There's not a lot to say about this reaction in terms of the bad guy except that he will react this way, too, if the response is triggered in him. Just be aware that it provides pretty good natural frontal protection so that if you are going to strike him with a baton, it is probably more likely to succeed if the strike is from the side—say to the leg—rather than directly up the middle.

DESTRUCTION OF BALANCE

Any time you take away someone's balance and he starts to fall or perceive that he is falling, he will try to recover his balance or break his fall. How does this apply to an attack scenario? Well, let's say for example that a 285 lb. drunken biker has gotten the drop on you and is "whaling" away on you. Let's say that he is throwing haymakers and you've gone into a defensive posture, "the cover," in boxing terms. How do you break the momentum of his attack? Let me give you several examples. In this instance, getting away (always choice #1) is not available.

You could dive in and grab his legs, getting both is the best, but one will do, and execute a double or single leg take down. You could lunge in and grab him around the waist, spinning violently to either side while pulling him down, or you could just try and defend against those punches and take a severe beating in the process. There is a myriad of ways to take another person off his feet. These could be any of the following: trips, throws, sweeps, reaps, pickups, or just a plain old football tackle. The results will always be the same in this case. The punching will stop. And now, since the bad guy will either be trying to stop you from taking him down, or breaking his fall, should you succeed, you will have broken his momentum and forced him to react to *you*. This now gives you the opportunity to wrest control of the situation. He will not allow his head or face to be planted into the concrete without trying to break his fall. This same principle applies when someone has grabbed you in a death grip, bear hug, or by the uniform. When he feels himself headed towards the blacktop, his grip will loosen.

PROTECTING THE EYES

You need your eyes. Human beings need eyesight to survive as a species. There is a huge portion of the brain dedicated to processing visual stimuli. There is a large portion of our survival mechanism devoted to protecting the eyes. Remember the startle response?

If you are attacked, let's say grabbed from behind and picked up for example, if possible attack the eyes with your fingers or any object, poking, stabbing, clawing, etc. It will have a profound effect on the bad guy. He will have to protect his eyes. Think of it like this. You might let me punch you hard in the shoulder. Would you let me, ever so lightly, just flick you in the eye? I won't even hit both eyes, just one. I promise, all you have to do is get at the eyes. If the bad guy has you bent backwards over the hood of your car in a strangle hold, and you can get a finger into his eyes, I guarantee you will be able to escape. The eyes are a soft target and no one, no matter how big or tough (barring psychotic drugs) can take a poke in the eyes and still fight effectively. Imagine someone jabbing at your eyes with a ballpoint pen. Do you think you're going to be trying to execute a wristlock or are you going to stop that pen from putting your eye out? It's so effective, yet very seldom used. The reason is that we are not dirty fighters and eye gouging is the ultimate in dirty fighting. Even in a fight to protect your daughter's honor, you wouldn't hesitate to break the guy's arm—but would you put his eye out? We, the good guys just don't think like that. I want you to be aware of this point, though. Not every poke in the eye puts someone's eye out. If it did, there would be a huge amount of one-eyed basketball players out there. However, if you've never been poked in the eye, I'll tell you this from first-hand experience, it stops you dead in your tracks until your vision recovers. Just striking towards the eyes without contacting them will produce a strong reaction in the opponent, often times enough to loosen a grip. If you do hit the eye, it's even better.

OBSTRUCTION OF AIRWAYS

How long can you hold your breath? One minute? Two minutes? Maybe three? All right now, give me 25 pushups, now while holding your breath give me 25 more pushups. Now how long can you hold your breath, ten seconds, fifteen seconds? Twenty seconds. By the time you get to ten seconds, each second seems like a minute. All you want to do is take a breath. Have you ever been in a near drowning situation? I have twice, once in an ice filled river and once in massive breakers off the California coast. I am here to tell you that there is nothing that creates the overwhelming panic and fear than being unable to take a breath causes. Because this is so primal a reaction, you can use it to great effect against an adversary. For example, you are in a wrestling match with an adversary and he has you clamped in a headlock where, because of his superior size or strength you are unable to escape. If you are able to reach around and cup your hand over his nose and mouth, you will elicit a reaction. You don't even need to run him out of breath. Just having something over the nose and mouth that interferes with breathing will cause him to weaken his hold, maybe cause him to break it if you have a good seal. Have someone cup their hand over your nose and mouth to experience how uncomfortable the feeling is. The first thing you want to do is just reach up and get that hand off your face.

You will elicit the same reaction by grabbing or encircling someone's throat and neck. When you start to execute a choke or strangle by putting your arm around an opponent's neck, you will start to get a reaction from him. If you succeed in getting the choke inserted and you get a seal on him, you will definitely get a reaction. Typically, he will reach up with both hands and try to pry your arm away. Unless he is a trained fighter, used to grappling, he will lose his offensive capability altogether and become completely defensive while trying to prevent the choke. Once again he is now reacting to you and this means you have broken his offensive momentum so he is no longer attacking.

ONE WEAPON - ONE STRIKE

There is a curious but real phenomenon that occurs whenever a person has a weapon in his hand. If the bad guy has a club in his hand, he will swing, throwing the same strike with the same hand over and over again. In fact in most fights, *real fights,* a person will often throw the same punch, say a right cross (his dominant hand), more likely a haymaker, over and over again. Now I know all the martial arts guys will say, "I'd be throwing kicks, punches, elbows *and* I'd be striking with the club. Well, I'm here to tell you that even "trained" fighters fall prey to this. I've been involved in the fight game for over 40 years in boxing, wrestling, jiu jitsu, Jeet Kune Do, and I've trained a lot of fighters. The hardest thing to teach a novice boxer to do is to throw combinations. He just wants to throw one punch at a time over and over again. I can take almost any student in class, put him in a sparring match and stick a rubber knife in his hand and guess what? No more kicks, no more punches, no head butts, no elbows, just the knife strike over and over again.

How can you make this work to your advantage? Well, thankfully most bad guys, even street fighters are not trained technicians and though they may have their tricks (usually getting in a sucker punch first) they are going to fall prey to this phenomenon almost every time. So if he's going to punch you, it will be with his right hand at least 85% of the time, since 85% of the population is right handed. If he has a weapon in his hand, 99% of the time it is held in his dominant hand so that is where the strike will come from. Further, having a weapon in his hand, will elicit the same strike with that weapon, over and over again. Not high, then low, not to the legs, then to the head, just the same over hand strike over and over again. He will not be throwing knees, elbows, punches, and kick combinations. Now knowing this allows you to pretty much know what he's going to do in advance. This gives you a tremendous advantage in defending and/or countering his attack.

Conversely, being aware of this phenomenon, you need to train to use **ALL** of your "weapons": punches, knees, kicks, elbows, etc., even if you are the one with a weapon in your hand. One of the drills I put our students through is one in which I give them a weapon and only allow them to use their off (non-weapon) hand. This drill along with a number of other sparring drills I've developed forces them out of the *one weapon* mindset and gets them to use all of the capabilities and "weapons" they have at their disposal.

In conclusion, these instinctive triggers I've just described do not represent techniques, and are not devastating or disabling in singular applications. We all know, the key to surviving a violent attack is to avoid or preempt if possible. If not, you then absorb the initial attack with the least damage to yourself and then immediately turn the tables so that the attacker is reacting to you and not you to him. This sounds great on paper, but in reality it is seldom by the book and is definitely not easy. You need to rely on all of your training, your skills and your wits to save your skin. Any fight is a game of chance and the way to win is to stack the odds in your favor. Being aware of and using these triggers is one of the tools that you can use along with all of your other training. It is a good way to keep some aces up your sleeve.

Chapter 3

Conditioning

"Fatigue makes cowards of us all."-- Vince Lombardi

Combat Conditioning

Why does physical conditioning play such a big part in the basic training of all military forces? Why does it play an even more important role in the training of elite special operations units, such as the Navy SEALS, Army Special Forces, Army Rangers and Marine Force Recon?

One of the primary reasons is because the quote at the top of the page by Vince Lombardi is very true. Physical fitness, extreme physical fitness, is primarily, a confidence builder. Knowing that you are physically fit and that your conditioning is the result of training so rigorous that out of 1000 able-bodied individuals only 100 would be able to make it through, is an *extreme* confidence builder. Knowing that no matter who you are up against in battle, whatever their level of fitness, confidence, or capability, you are better in all regards (gives you tremendous psychological power). And remember, *power perceived is power achieved*. When you train individuals for teams that will be placed in the most extreme conditions, under the highest levels of stress imaginable, you want to give them all the advantages that you can, to always tip the scales in their favor. Extreme physical fitness is an integral part of that package. And it has been that way since professional soldiers began organized training over 5000 years ago.

What is combat conditioning? I define combat conditioning as three parts of a whole, those individual parts being equal measures of **strength, power, and endurance**. Let's look at those three parts separately.

1. Strength is being the ability to lift, move, or carry heavy objects. In other words this would be akin to the abilities of a weightlifter who has developed muscular strength above the norm in order to lift heavier weights.

2. Power is the ability to use that strength at a high capacity over a sustained period of time. This would be like the power needed by a wrestler who has to use his strength at near capacity over a sustained length of time, or perhaps that of a *gandydancer*, a railroad worker who replaces the steel rails of the railroad track. I worked on a railroad steel gang for two years. I know all about sustained strength over a long period of time. We worked replacing rails, 12 hour days, rain or shine.

3. **Endurance** is the ability to keep going and going and going – just like the Energizer Bunny. In this case endurance means being able to travel over long distances, up to 20 miles under a 60 to 90 pound pack and still be able to engage in the fight, or in the case of the Navy SEALs, a 20 mile swim. This is the marathon aspect of conditioning.

The key to combat conditioning is striking a balance between all three which produces a result we will call *functional conditioning*. Functional conditioning is having the optimal amount of strength, power, and endurance to perform at your ultimate level of operation or function to accomplish your goal or task. This may not mean that you can deadlift 600 pounds, but it does mean that you can carry 200 pounds for a quarter of a mile. Both of these require great strength, but the first one is explosive and brief and the other is continuous over time and distance. That in a nutshell is the difference between brute strength and *functional strength*. Similarly, if you look at long-distance runners or marathoners, they are almost always rail thin. Yes, they are in great cardiovascular shape – for running long distances, but they're not very strong and do not possess explosive power or the ability to sustain such power over time. For truly functional combat conditioning, you need to take the strength of a power lifter, the sustained power of a wrestler, and the endurance of a marathoner, then strike a balance among all three to find and reach your own ultimate potential of *functional combat conditioning*. This will involve perhaps, a different approach to training than you're already doing and I guarantee that if you're serious about real functional strength and combat conditioning, you'll be doing the hardest and most grueling training that you have ever done. How do we accomplish this? Well there's way too much material to go into here, but I will give you some sources. CrossFit training is a pretty good place to start. Look for a CrossFit training center near you. Most MMA gyms have pretty good functional training programs. A good boxing gym is a great training choice and most now offer auxiliary training and conditioning along with a boxing workout. By the way, a heavy bag training routine is great. As to setting up your own programs there are several books I recommend.

1. *Chain Reaction Training* - Ernest Emerson - available at Emersonknives.com and TheGuardianShepherd.com

2. *Never Let Go* - Dan John

3. *Kettlebell, Simple & Sinister* - Pavel Tsatsouline

4. *Kettlebell Conditioning System* - Steve Maxwell

5. *Heavy Bag Training* - Sammy Franco

6. *Navy SEAL Fitness* - Stewart Smith

All of these books offer great information, a huge number of exercise training guides and inspiration. I recommend you get them all. I'll close this chapter with two mantras from Emerson Combat System training classes that I want you to take to heart: **"You'll never run me out of gas,"** and my favorite quote **"Train like a madman... Fight like a demon!"**

Chapter 4.

Awareness

The cornerstone of pre-emptive self-defense

The key to avoiding conflict before it starts is being aware of your surroundings at all times. In the tactical world of the operator it is called *Situational Awareness*. That is, being aware of your situation in relationship to your environment at all times. In the tactical sense, situational awareness is defined as, *a state of general alertness which allows you to take away the element of surprise from the threat.*

We are going to talk about several things in this chapter including the three states of vigilance and preparedness to act, and also Colonel Jeff Cooper's color code system of awareness. We'll start with the three states of vigilance as seen from an operator's point of view. In this case I will use a military patrol as a vehicle to illustrate the progression of the three states.

Relaxed Vigilance – This is a general radar scanning, looking for anything out of the normal.

Heightened Vigilance – Something has caught your eye, or seems out of place, just not right, you take notice of it and observe, and you keep your eye on it.

Hypervigilance – Danger, threat or bad guys are detected and you are keying off their actions.

To illustrate: you are about to go on patrol in enemy territory. You are assigned to move from point A to Z and are to engage any enemy activity in the area. You are in a state of *relaxed vigilance* as you leave point A and start moving into Indian Territory. You are alert and scanning the environment, on the lookout for anything out of place. As you progress farther, you find a flattened area in the grass, a sure sign that someone has recently been in the area. Everyone in the patrol automatically switches to a state of *heightened vigilance,* because you don't know if the enemy has passed through five hours ago or five minutes ago. At this point, everyone is actively scanning and listening for anything that might signal that others are in your immediate proximity. Then suddenly, you see movement through the woods and hear hushed voices. At this point you and everyone else switch to a state of *hyper-vigilance* in which you are now aware of the enemy and must maintain your own concealment while observing the enemy's movement and intentions. Your actions are now in essence interacting and keying off the actions of the enemy without their knowledge. This requires the utmost of vigilance and caution. And sure enough, you find out that they are setting up an ambush, perhaps for you. So you react by setting up a counter ambush and seek to catch them by surprise.

"He who strikes first usually wins" – Ernest Emerson

There are several components or evolutions of pre-emptive self-defense. Some of these are so obvious they could be called just plain old common sense. Some others are much more subtle and require an ability to read a situation and adjust or modify your role in the interaction and/or manipulate the behavior of the attackers or bad guy to your advantage.

Detect-Deny-Destroy

These three words precisely sum up the essential objectives of what the concept of *pre-emptive self-defense* is all about. These three objectives, the same objectives used to protect us from terrorist attacks, are as effective for personal self-protection as they are when used in protecting our country.

There are several steps you can take to make them work just as effectively for you.

You may have already seen the material in this section discussed in previous books that I have written, but it is so important that I have chosen to include them in this book since it is included in all of my lectures and seminars. In case you are not familiar with my other work, here it is.

The Color Code of Awareness

This is the color code system that define the levels of mental preparedness as defined by Colonel Jeff Cooper, perhaps the greatest influence on modern gun fighting and the teaching of shooting skills, of the 20th century. Colonel Cooper devised a way to quantify and categorize the different states of mental preparedness that you are in, from a completely relaxed, unaware state of mind, to the state of mind needed to engage in lethal action.

He developed a color code of White, Yellow, Orange and Red and used it to describe the escalating states of self-preparedness.

There has been a lot written about Colonel Jeff Cooper's color code system and the conditions of awareness. This system has been successfully taught to and used by Military, Law Enforcement and civilians for decades. Basically, the origin of the color code system is that Colonel Cooper deduced that there were four levels of awareness that constantly affect us as human beings and that we are always in one of those conditions. Further, they will definitely affect your ability to survive a life threatening crisis or event, depending on which condition you are in at the onset of the event. In order to teach these conditions by describing them separately and in an understandable manner to military recruits during their training, he assigned a color code to each of the four conditions or levels of awareness. These conditions are as follows: Here in the words of Colonel Cooper are the conditions:

1. Condition White -You are unprepared and unready to take lethal action. If you are attacked in condition white you will probably die unless your adversary is totally inept.

2. Condition Yellow -You bring yourself to the understanding that your life may be in danger and you may have to do something about it.

3. Condition Orange - You have determined upon a specific adversary and are prepared to take action, which may result in his death, but you are not in a lethal mode.

4. Condition Red -You are in a lethal mode and will shoot if circumstances warrant it.

Now the same conditions as I interpret and teach in class:

1. Condition White -You are awake but not paying attention to your surroundings or environment.

2. Condition Yellow-You are paying attention to your situational awareness, surroundings, environment, and are aware and assessing others in your vicinity for potential threats to your safety.

3. Condition Orange-You have positively identified a threat and are actively formulating a countermeasure and response.

4. Condition Red-You are actively responding to the threat which now has you engaged in combat - the fight.

By identifying these different conditions as differing states of readiness and becoming consciously aware of them, you can assess what condition you are in at any given moment and decide if it is appropriate. It also gives you the ability to make a conscious decision to step to the next rung of readiness if the situation warrants.

So, let's start with the most obvious ways to protect yourself from an attack and hopefully, pre-empt an attack.

You must be aware. Your best defense against being caught in a terrorist attack, being caught off guard, is to not ever let your guard down. In operator's language this is called situational awareness, and what it means is maintaining a 360 degree awareness of your environment and everyone who is in, enters or leaves that environment. Generally this circle extends out 20-30 feet from you at its center. Being aware of building and room entrances and exits is a must and of course all choke points and dead ends that you should avoid. Practice reading people as an art form. Look for nervousness, suspicious behavior, strange dress (coats in warm weather) and backpacks, suitcases, or bags left unattended. The art of situational awareness is always a work in progress. It is something that has to be practiced to become effective, to be "switched on," as the Brits say. The bottom line in situational awareness is that you never want to be the one who says, "I never saw it coming." Now bear in mind that situational awareness is only valid if your interpretation of circumstances, situations and individuals is correct. So you need to understand a couple of things. You are a product of your own background, your upbringing, your life experience, and your personal philosophy of life. If you are someone who has lived a sheltered life, never exposed to harsh realities or shielded from the truth, you are going to have a different "view" of people than a 25-year-old veteran patrol officer. It's not right or wrong it's just a fact. Of these two who do you think is going to be more situationally aware? More suspicious? The point is that we actually have all the same "antennae" as that veteran cop. It's only a matter of how you interpret what you see or feel. So you need to listen to your senses and your gut feel. If it doesn't "feel" right-it's not right. Just don't override your own self-protective resources.

Let me give you an example. People are in a mall and someone opens fire with a gun. Afterward, during interviews, some people say, "I heard pop, pop, pop. I thought someone was lighting off firecrackers." Now, I ask, have you ever been in a mall where someone lit off a bunch of firecrackers? I haven't. So why would you think it would be firecrackers? I'm not saying it has never happened. I'm just not aware of it. But, I have heard of someone going into a mall and shooting people with a firearm. I'm also sure that most have also heard of that. If a Marine just back from Afghanistan was in that mall do you think he would have thought those pops were firecrackers? I'd go with him covering his family and looking for cover. What would you do? I'm going to finish this section with one bit of sage advice and I'm going to ask you not to question it-just believe it. When you're out in the general public, there are only two people that will look you directly in the eyes: cops and bad guys. So if someone is looking directly back at you, you're going to have to figure out which of those he is.

Chapter 5.
Mindset

Developing the warrior's mindset

Developing the proper mindset is also one of the primary goals of all military training. Just like physical conditioning, it is taken to the extreme in the training of all special operations personnel as well as in the training of all CIA Officers, especially the training of their Special Activities Division, SAD. This is especially necessary in terms of small unit activities or operations where sometimes a single operator is tasked with a mission. When you are directing a large number of men such as a battalion, it is important that all of the soldiers take the proper mindset into battle. After all, there are two things that are infectious on the field of combat: cowardice and courage. So you want and hope your soldiers have the correct mindset. However, when small units are involved, such as a 12 man platoon, or a three or four man insertion team is deployed, it is absolutely imperative that *no one* becomes the weak link, since there is so much essential inter-dependency on fellow teammates to do the job they are assigned. In large-scale operations a single individual has less effect individually, since their actions are buoyed up by dozens if not hundreds of other soldiers. So in terms of individuals, it is extremely important to strengthen the will and harden the resolve of every operator, every warrior, to the degree that they will never quit, never give up, and never accept failure or defeat. This process is accomplished through a series of physical and mental tests designed to push the individual past all previous limits that they thought they had. In addition they are continuously forced to do difficult tasks and make complex decisions under the extremes of stress, chaos, and confusion. Marine Corps basic training is probably one of the most effective and recognizable examples of this process through which a common man is transformed into a warrior.

What are those traits, those characteristics that define us as a warrior? What makes a warrior different from those who are not? Well, the first and by far the most important is that a warrior is ready and willing to go into harm's way for a righteous or noble cause, or to protect those who may be in danger. The key to the proper mindset is to give you the best mental or psychological skills to do so, when *you* hear the call to arms.

One of the necessary components to being mentally prepared is the ability to make quick decisions, quicker than the bad guys. It is a matter of when attacked, to be able to switch from a defensive mode (reactive) to an offensive mode (active) as quickly as possible. In order to do so efficiently you have to be prepared before you go into action. In order to do that you must develop a *mental trigger* that when pulled, propels you automatically into action. This means that you need to prepare for the worst and hope for the best. What I mean by this is that most people are oblivious to potential threats and dangerous situations even as they are unfolding before their very eyes. This occurs because luckily, most of us never come face-to-face with extreme violence. And in part this is because the laws and mores, the structures of our society protect us to a large degree from harm and danger. And as a whole, the system seems to be working pretty well. It is also a fact that most of the violence we see or experience is on the news or happening to a fictional character in the fantasyland of the movies or on TV. In other words it always happens to someone else. So it is only natural that the immediate mental reaction that most people experience when confronted with a violent attack is, "This can't be happening to me." That is why it is very common for people to make the statement after an attack, "I never saw it coming." You can never let that be *your* mental attitude. It is the reason why most of the victims that are killed in a violent act get killed. They never even get the chance to fight back. Those victims carried the mindset, "It can't happen to me" (violence) which then becomes, "I can't believe it's happening to me," and ends with an obituary notice.

So having a mental trigger, being set to go into action when needed requires a shift in attitude. That shift goes like this. Your mindset needs to shift from, "It can't happen to me," or "I never saw it coming," to "It can happen to me. I expect it. I have a plan and I will follow through aggressively, ruthlessly and without mercy to execute it – without hesitation." That is the *mental trigger*.

An undercover counterterrorist operator from the Israeli Duv Devan unit named Garrett told me one time, "Once a warrior has decided he will react to the situation, he transforms into a machine. He is moving like a pre-programmed robot that does his job without hesitation and without emotion until it is finished."

The attitude and mindset shared by all special operation warriors and the one you need to embrace is simply this. *I have the willingness to do whatever is needed, refusing in advance to become a victim, and I will never, ever give up.*

In regard to the power of attitude and mindset any operator will tell you that they would rather go into battle alongside a weak man with a warrior's attitude than alongside a strong man with a weak attitude. One will fight to the bitter end and the other will crumble at the time when they are needed the most. You must be the warrior that never crumbles.

Chapter 6.

Goals

How do you get from here to there?

Of course you can prepare. You can practice. You can learn all you want, spending countless hours, months, and years, getting ready. Getting ready for what? Why am I doing all of this? The general idea why one would do all of this is simply to be prepared. But for me anyway I am also doing it because I love it. And I'm also doing it so I can teach others. I'm doing it so I can protect my family and brothers that need it. But I will also tell you that I wasted a lot of time on things I didn't need, on things that wouldn't work, and countless things that sidetracked me along the way. The reason was that I did not have a clearly defined set of goals. And then a mentor of mine showed me the value of goals, and it changed my life. Once you have a set of goals, clearly defined goals, along with time limits and mileposts, things really start to happen. The best thing about all of this is that the simple program I'm about to outline for you works for business, for sports, for education, for marriage and for training. In short this works for life. When I was in my teens and twenties I had a lot of heroes and role models that I looked up to in sports such as baseball, football, martial arts, boxing, and in education, politics and history. In short I was inspired by their greatness and I wanted to emulate them. And being interested in all these iconic figures led me to studying them and reading about them. What I found out was that many of them shared common obvious traits such as dedication, focus, and discipline. But what stuck out to me was that most of them had set goals and schedules that they religiously and tirelessly adhered to. They were committed to getting the results they were after. Many of them kept records and some set up their daily schedules the night before as to what they wanted to accomplish each day. Along with their overall long-term *wants*, they used those schedules to keep on track and also to gauge their progress towards those ends. When I adopted their methods I started to see better results. Then in my late twenties I became good friends with a Navy SEAL who taught me many things, one of which was a program for success based on a simple formula of setting goals. It included short-term goals, midterm goals, and long-term goals. The formula was simple and it quickly became one of my *good* habits. I will now pass it on to you. Here is that simple formula for success:

First, set your goals – What do you want to be? What do you want to do? What do you want to accomplish? These will fall into short-term, midterm, and long-term goals.

Second; set realistic mileposts for your progress.

Third; ask the question, does my behavior support my goals? If your behavior matches your goals then you are on the right track. If you are doing things that do not support your goals or something that may be preventing your progress, then you must modify your behavior to support your goals. This will involve sacrifice, dedication, and the stern will of discipline. For example, if I really loved smoking cigarettes but wanted to be a marathon runner, I would have to quit smoking, thereby modifying my behavior to support my goals.

Although this seems like a simple formula for success, it requires some serious soul-searching, objective self-evaluation, and a dedicated effort to produce the correct results. Certainly it not as hard on paper as it is in practice. However, as hard as it might be to get the program started, once it becomes your routine for tackling any goal or problem, it then becomes a habit, and that is when it becomes easy.

Once this goal setting process becomes your habit and you start to see the results then you'll never want to tackle any task or do things any other way. It's that successful. Let's look at how this applies in terms of *training to survive inside the kill zone.*

My goals in this book are these:

1. Preemptive self-defense - *short-term goal*

2. Survival in combat – *midterm goal*

3. Destruction of the enemy, opponent – *long-term goal*

The purpose of this book is about constructing and rearranging your behavior to support the goals I have just outlined.

Chapter 7

Capability and Capacity

You know how to do it, but will you do it?

Many people spend years training to be a shooter or a fighter, enduring hours of sacrifice, the pain of injuries, breaks and bruises. And as a result they become very proficient in the skill set of bringing death and destruction upon another human being. Yet some at that very moment when all those skills are needed the most, fail to execute. They either go into a fugue state or perform so weakly that although being more skilled than their opponent, they get overwhelmed by the actions of the bad guys. In the law enforcement community there is a phenomenon called a *hesitation shooting*. What this describes is a situation where an officer encounters a bad guy with a gun. It may even be during the commission of a crime in progress or perhaps even a *shots fired* call, so the officer already knows there are bad guys and bad behavior in play. The officer comes onto a bad guy with a gun who points it directly at the officer in a threatening manner. The officer also has his gun drawn and pointed at the suspect. The suspect fires his weapon and kills the officer. The officer never pulls his trigger. The question is always, "Why didn't the officer shoot? He had the capability and every right to shoot, and yet he didn't." There are of course many possible answers to that single question. The first answer is that the suspect was a bad guy and the officer was a good guy. Maybe *too* good. It is not in our nature as *good guys* to kill someone. The suspect was already a bad guy and had probably shot someone else previously. It was in his nature to kill. *For more insight on the nature of criminal sociopathic behavior, read my article on the subject, *"Know Who You're Up Against,"* located at:

Emersonknives.com or TheGuardianshepherd.com.

It's as simple as the statement, "Bad guys do bad things and good guys don't do bad things." How does this apply to the subject of this book, "Surviving Inside the Kill Zone?" It has everything to do with surviving a deadly attack.

What it comes down to is this. Up to this point everything you have done, your training and everything we've discussed here has to do with **capability**--The skills needed to carry out an act. The final piece in the puzzle is **capacity,** the act of *using* all those skills against another human being without hesitation, trepidation, or remorse.

Now we can all fantasize about wreaking havoc on another human, stabbing him or even shooting him, but are you actually ready to do so to the full extent of your capabilities if it results in the death of another human being? What if that means doing horrible things to accomplish the act? Will you rip someone's face open? Will you gouge someone's eye out? Do you have the capacity to tear out someone's trachea with your teeth? Do you have the capacity to bend his arm backwards until you feel it cracking, breaking or pulling out of the joint, even as you hear him screaming in agony? Well you'd better, because remember that the premise of this entire discussion is about how to survive a *deadly attack*. What that means is that unless you are willing to do these things to the bad guy, he's going to do them to you and then your wife and then to your daughter or son. If you're in this situation, (and remember this is not a "I'm going to kick your ass," posturing of two young stallions) this is a bad guy, a killer who has broken into your house, a shooter at the mall, or perhaps a terrorist intent on killing as many innocents as possible and about to send himself to hell. In this case it then becomes a requirement that you have to do anything and everything possible to stop him.

You need to think about this long before you might ever need to use your skills, your capability. And that time to think is right now. You need to mentally cross that bridge before you ever get to that bridge. I'm assuming that those of you that are reading this book fall into the good guy category, so it's not in your nature to be comfortable when causing pain and injury to another person. That's a good thing. But when and if you ever run into a situation where you are facing such violence, you have to be able to become that bad person that we all have learned not to be.

When another human being has made a decision, to bring violence and destruction against you, your loved ones or any other innocent victims, then he is no longer a human being, he is the enemy. And the enemy deserves no mercy. General George Patton said the following, "May God have mercy on my enemies for I will not." It is that foregone conclusion that allows you to act without hesitation and with singular focus in eliminating the threat.

When someone has decided to hurt or kill innocent victims, then in my book he has forfeited his rights as a human being. In order to act effectively, decisively and with conviction, you cannot personalize the perpetrator, the attacker, the enemy. In a deadly attack the situation becomes a zero sum game. A gain for one must result in a loss for the other. In the game of life and death, many times for one to live, another must die. Fellow instructor and author Rory Miller puts it into terms we can all relate to: "Make my kids orphans or make his kids orphans? That's a no-brainer."

We must all live with our choices and the consequences of our actions. In order to do so you must have moral clarity. Here's how I look at it. The Eighth Commandment is usually stated as, "Thou shall not kill." Studying the early interpretations of the Ten Commandments, I believe the eighth commandant was originally interpreted as and should still be read as "Thou shall not commit murder." There's a big difference between murder, the unjustified taking of innocent life and the taking of a life to save the lives of others, a justified act. About this, I have perfect, crystal-clear moral clarity. If someone forces me to have to take their life then it's on them, not me. They caused it and *they* forced *my* hand. I won't lose one minute of sleep over that.

There are times when I'm asked to give lectures to police departments and military groups. We reach this section of the lecture on capability and capacity and moral clarity and I use the following: As a sniper you might get called out to a situation where there is a hostage and a bad guy threatening to take a hostage's life. You are given the order to take the shot and do. Afterwards if you need to go to six months of psychological therapy, then you're not a sniper, you're just a good shot. A sniper kills bad guys and they deserve to die. A guy with a gun to a child's head deserves what he gets, there is no guilt in that. And the only drinking I'm driven to do as a result, is when my buddies and I drink a shot of Jack to toast a clean shot and a righteous kill later that evening. Don't get me wrong, it's not a celebration of death nor glorifying the taking of a human life. It's about doing the right thing, a very hard thing and taking responsibility for its consequences. But it's so that others may live. That's moral clarity.

"People sleep soundly in their beds at night because rough men stand ready to do violence on their behalf." That is moral clarity as stated by George Orwell.

So the bottom line is this. *Capability needs Capacity* to work. In the real arena of combat where any hesitation, mistake or second thought can mean the difference between taking the trip home or taking a trip to the morgue, both have to function at full power with no encumbrances. You must have the willingness to execute your skills with violence of action.

Japanese samurai who faced death every time they fought, called it *a loss of self*. A state where "I" does not exist. The only thing that exists is my purpose and the enemy. "I" am merely a vehicle used to carry out my purpose against the enemy. In that state of mind there is no regard for safety or welfare, no hesitation, no thoughts, and only the singular focus to destroy the enemy. For if "I" do not exist, I cannot be hurt and I cannot lose. Also in that state of mind, the enemy becomes not a man but merely an obstacle to overcome. Such is the *Warrior's* view of life-and-death combat. For you to survive, it must also be yours.

Conclusion

This book is the result of numerous requests over the years by people who attended a lecture or seminar I have given all over the world titled "Surviving Inside the Kill Zone." Just as in a two-hour seminar, I'm not here to teach you fighting techniques to use against an opponent. This book is not that type of instructional vehicle either. Quite frankly, no matter what some authors or instructors might tell you, you cannot learn to fight from a book. But you can learn a great deal about *how* to fight from a book. What I mean by that is that fighting is not just *physical*, it is also *mental*. In fact the best fighters have always been the best thinkers. They are the survivors, the aces, the sergeants, the chiefs, the champions, and the leaders. They survived to pass on their knowledge because they knew what to do, when to do it, how to do it, and why to do it.

As much as this book is about fighting and human combat, it would be of more value and honor to me if it *kept* you from ever having to engage in combat. That would always be the ultimate goal, as it should be for any teacher or instructor. But for those that by chance, circumstance, or choice are caught in harm's way, the goal of this book is that the principles and attributes that are described herein, coupled with your own skills and survival instincts act to help tip the odds in your favor. In this arena, you want every advantage you can bring into play against the evil that you confront.

I hope that you understand that all of the seven chapters are written to support your ability to "Fight the good fight," and stop evil dead in its tracks. If only one thing in this book helps enable you to do so, when and if that time ever comes, then I will consider my efforts here a success.

In the end, I cannot train you to be a fighter. I can only train you how to train to be a fighter. The real hard work is now up to you.

Good luck and Godspeed.

Ernest Emerson

Bonus Chapter

Thank you for reading this book. I have included as a bonus for you, the first chapter of one of my other books for you to read. If you are interested you can find this book along with all my others to purchase at Amazon.com or for an autographed copy, you can order directly off of the website, TheGuardianShepherd.com

Bonus Articles

As an extra bonus I've also included here two articles from my website TheGuardianShepherd.com, where you will find dozens of free articles and information concerning counter-terrorist training and tactics, personal security, personal family safety, training, conditioning, and self defense. You will also be able to download lectures, seminars and training routines to give you the tools, skills and mentality needed to be the most effective "Guardian Shepherd" for yourself, your family, your loved ones, and others who might need your protection in a time of crisis.

BONUS CHAPTER

from

Chain Reaction Training

Chapter 1

Fall In Love with the Process of Becoming Great

Welcome to the world of combat strength and fitness. It is a world where optimal fitness and functional strength are not for the sake of fitness or strength alone. To a soldier they are their tools, just as a helmet, body armor, knife and rifle are their tools. Like those tools, combat strength and fitness are just as necessary to save your life in combat. Since you know that you must keep your gear and weapons in top working order, so it is also with your fitness and strength. I could give you a million reasons why you need fitness to survive in combat and another million reasons why you need strength to survive in combat. But I'm going to tell you it's not the obvious reasons that I know you're thinking about: "I'm going to kick some bad guy's ass!" I want you to think about this: what if you had to run a quarter-mile to tear one of your teammates out of a downed Helo, then hoist him onto your back and carry him a quarter-mile back to cover? Could you do that? Can you do that? If I was the guy in the downed Helo, I surely hope you could.

So now you're telling me you're not a soldier, a cop or fireman. Why do you need this high degree of elite warrior's fitness? Honestly, I don't know why you would need it, but I'll tell you why I need it and that's because in an emergency, a fight, or to protect my loved ones, I would have it. If I were to fail, it would not be because I ran out of steam. The ability to survive in combat or any emergency situation is governed by your ability to control as many factors as possible in an out of control situation. Training in the skills of such things as marksmanship and all the other combat related skills allow you to have as much control as you can wrest through the practice of those skills prior to having to use them in actual combat. You should look at physical conditioning as a requisite skill that can always count on and should never be a factor that would fail you in a time of need.

Hard physical training, and I mean real hard, gut wrenching, sweat dripping training is a learning experience. This isn't just about being in shape. You can join a local fitness center, work a couple of weight machines, and jump on an elliptical machine for 15 minutes. You may get "in shape" according to the "average" standard. But it's not going be a learning experience. What do I mean by that? First off, I don't want to be average, and the average man never knows how far you can really go. When you push yourself to your limit only to realize that you're only half way through the training session, you're about to learn a lot about yourself. Am I a quitter? Is this really all I've got? Really? Am I "average?" You have to answer those questions for yourself. The answers you find will reveal a lot to you about yourself. And it will teach you things you cannot learn until you actually face them. For example, how will you ever know whether you are a quitter or not until you face a situation where you think you can't go on; not one inch farther, a place where you can either give up and quit or reach down deep within and push on? Are you a quitter? Honestly, are you a quitter? How would you know? I'll tell you something. Every single candidate who starts BUDs/SEAL training would tell you that he is not a quitter. Yet out of the 150 plus students that start every BUD/S class, about 100 quit every time. And these are guys who knew that they wanted to be a Navy SEAL since they were 12 years old. So in order to "find" yourself and your limits, you have to push harder than you have ever pushed yourself before. And then you have to push harder.

There's more. Once you've pushed past your quitting point and realize that now that limit is gone, gone forever, you now know that you can go further than you thought you could. And it feels great. Breaking these barriers is the first step in learning that there really are no barriers, that all of your limits are self-imposed. You'll learn that if you set the limit, hell yes, you can break the limit. When you believe, truly believe, that you have no limits; the world opens up its doors for you. That's when you realize that you can do anything you set your mind on doing. Anything. You are anything but average. A friend of mine told me once, "Ernest, the world is run by "C" students." I'm going to ask you this. Do you want to just be a "C" student or do you want to be a "B" or maybe an "A" student? Did you answer yes to that question? Not me. I said no. I want to be a triple AAA +++ student. Being good at something is one thing. Being great at something requires several essential elements: extreme goals, extreme efforts, and extreme confidence. It's about developing habits, good habits, not bad habits, developing the habit of never settling for anything less than excellence, the habit of never quitting and the habit of never, ever giving up. There are few ways on earth to learn these things and develop these habits better than through extreme physical training. The elite military units also know this.

Part of the reason that Navy SEAL training is so tough is to take the candidates beyond their physical limits. It then tests their will to continue, the resolve to never quit. Because if you quit in training, how could you ever be trusted to not quit in combat?

One of the other reasons is to stress your body and mind by using grueling physical workouts and then creating a situation where you are forced to face a decision-making process. This will tell how well you can make decisions while under stress and the pain of physical exhaustion.

And another reason of course is to build you into one of the most physically fit human beings on earth. Functional, combat fitness is again a necessary ingredient for actual combat. If you run out of steam, your mission will fail, or you or your teammates will be killed. Legendary Green Bay Packers coach Vince Lombardi once said, "Fatigue makes cowards of us all," and if you are a member of a SEAL Team, you don't want to be that guy. Along with this elite physical fitness is the building of a supreme confidence, knowing you are better than the rest. When you are sending a warrior into combat, confidence is an absolute requirement.

BONUS ARTICLE 1 of 2

How to Knock Someone Out With One Punch

Everything you ever needed to know how to knock someone out with one punch you learned in your high school physics class. Don't get caught up in any of the hocus pocus mumbo jumbo that is so pervasive in most martial arts systems. It's really all about physics, almost.

What we'll do here is break down the knockout punch into its 5 basic components. By dividing the power punch into these 5 individual components we can look at each one as a separate and **trainable** attribute that you can work on individually to dramatically increase your punching power, effectiveness and your ability to knock someone out with one punch.

I'm going to use boxers to illustrate these points since, well, boxing is all about punching. Some boxers have it some don't have it. What is it? The explosive power to knock someone completely off their feet. The power to hit someone in the head and hurt them in their toes. The explosiveness to jar your fillings loose. That is the power knockout punch.

Why do some boxers have it and some don't? After all, in a bout the combatants are matched to the same general size and most of the time virtually the exact weight. They are both using the same skill set and tactics, yet one of them knocks opponents out fight after fight and the other only rarely does so. I have found that there were several things that the heavy hitters all had in common.

These are the ingredients that are needed to hit hard – real hard.

I have broken down the whole into 5 absolutely essential attributes that can be taught to others or enhanced in yourself that will increase your power dramatically. They are as follows;

1. **Body Mechanics** – You **must** have proper body mechanics. Most martial artists and many boxers have poor to marginal body mechanics. Without going into too much detail, proper body mechanics must include footwork, **violent** hip rotation, proper shoulder/arm position and correct fist/wrist/arm alignment. However, the most important aspect of proper body mechanics is

efficiency of motion and economy of action. In other words, no unnecessary motion or muscular action. Think of it as your entire body being relaxed and **only** the muscles and motion needed to deliver the action (in this case a punch) are activated.

2. **Speed** – This is the simplest to understand and yet, maybe the most difficult to execute. It's really simple physics here guys. Newton's 2nd Law. Acceleration times mass equals force. The faster your punch travels the more power it generates. Now most people assume they are born with a certain speed. "I wish I could be as fast as John. John is just naturally fast." Well, the truth is, you **are** born with a certain speed. That speed is as fast as any other human who has ever walked the face of this earth. You just have to realize it. The activation of the muscle cells used to move the arm or any part of the body is the result of an electrochemical reaction. It travels at a fixed rate just like electricity or the speed of light. Barring some physiological abnormality or disease, your ability to activate your muscles is just as fast as the fastest person you have ever seen or admired.

However, if you are a slow thinker or a slow reactor (mentally) then you will never be able to realize your full speed potential because your thinking will be a beat or two behind your opponent. In order to be fast – real fast – you also need to start training your mind to start thinking faster. You have to look at speed thinking just like speed reading. The faster you force yourself to read, the faster you can read. It's not just your arms or legs, your brain has to start moving faster also. Now, having stated the above, there are two **key** elements to increasing your speed. You gotta **believe**, brother. You have to start thinking and convincing yourself that you are the fastest human being that ever lived – ever, and you have to start thinking fast. I mean believe it – no self doubts – **none**. The second key element is that you have to start moving fast, punching fast – **punching faster**. Now I know it's a little different when I'm standing in front of you screaming Punch fast. Faster! Faster damn it! But you have to push yourself on this one. This is where the proper body mechanics start to become evident. You can't be fast if you're out of balance or clumsy. Remember efficiency of action, economy of motion? You can't be fast if you're all tensed up and adding any unnecessary motion to your effort. Think of a world-class 100-meter sprinter. He practices sprinting, not jogging. He practices sprinting at **full** speed. There are dozens of drills and exercises to increase or enhance speed but the most important, really, is convincing yourself that you are that fast. If you can do that, the rest starts to fall into place by itself.

3. **Accuracy** – All the power in the world is nothing if you can't put it where you want. The most powerful gun in the world is useless if it cannot hit the target. Punching power is really all about the transfer of energy. The more energy I can deliver to a target the more efficient and effective I am. One thing you will notice is that, as your speed increases, your accuracy will decline. You must practice accuracy drills at full speed to increase your accuracy at full speed. It's just that simple. There are lots of accuracy drills, but here is my personal favorite. Hang a piece of paper with a small black circle on it about the size of a ping pong ball or smaller. Hang it so it's suspended at

about chin level and practice finger jabs or punches at full speed against it. I hang it taped to the end of a chain so it returns faster. Concentrate on moving at full ultimate speed and centering the target. It will come with practice and you will see improvement the more you do it.

4. **Timing** – You have to put your punch where the target is – not where it was. Think of it like leading a duck with a shotgun. You're not shooting where the duck is, you're shooting where the duck will be. Timing is not accuracy. Accuracy is accuracy. In simple terms, timing is accurate estimation and timing is experience. Timing is developed by sparring. It is developed by training against an individual who is moving in a spontaneous and unrehearsed manner.

5. **Mental Intensity** – This is when it gets a little voodoo. You may know by now that I don't believe in secret powers or any of that hocus pocus. But, there is one component in developing ultimate punching power that I consider the only x factor. You have to want to hit hard, to hit harder than you ever have before. Every time you train, every

time you punch I want you to punch harder than you ever thought you did before. You have to **hit to hurt**, plain and simple.

There are plenty of exercises and drills that you can do that will enhance your power but really the best – **the best** - is to stand toe to toe with a heavy bag and hit it like you want to rip it from the ceiling. The heavy bag is the only place you can really hit something as hard as humanly possible. And that is what you have to do. Hit the bag as hard as humanly possible. You can hit much harder that you think you can – really. **But, you have to do it.** It's the same principle as when a spotter can scream at you to put that weight up, to grind out that last rep. Something, someone has to push you to go a little harder. You have to be that someone. You have to hit harder, Harder! HARDER! Yes, I know you can sacrifice speed by trying to emphasize power. But that's for the amateurs. A huge lumbering thump of a punch is not what I'm talking about here. I'm talking about having a grenade detonate every time your fist strikes the bag. And I'm talking about a grenade thrown by your arm with the speed of lightning. Therein lies the difference, a big difference.

Mike Tyson said it in absolutely the best way I've ever heard it described. When asked early in his career about his incredible string of knockouts, he simply said, "You have to throw your punches with **bad intent**."

Bear in mind though, that you will need all of the other attributes to fully make use of true mental intensity and see its results. At the same time, you could fully develop all of the first four attributes but still not experience your ultimate potential, if you don't add the magic ingredient, "Bad Intent". You will need the correct body mechanics, speed, accuracy and timing. Leave any of them out and you won't be able to hit the bag as hard as you want and you will feel it.

The last thing I will cover is really not an attribute it is the target. Now in terms of human physiology, a knockout (loss of consciousness) is simply a rattling of the brain, i.e. the brain hitting the inside of the skull. Brain trauma = concussion.

There are several ways to make this happen but in terms of human anatomy the easiest way is to effect "a violent side to side rotation of the head." In other words a good shot right to the jaw. It can be straight on or better yet, to either side of the chin. This is the one punch that puts most fighters on the canvas no matter how big or how strong. I would call it the #1 target for a knockout punch. Targeting is really where timing and accuracy become so important.

But in the end I want you to understand that it is very hard to "just knock someone out." Outside of the "sucker punch", you only get the chance to hit your target when it is there and it's not there for very long. That's why flurries often result in a knockout. One punch finally gets through, but when it does you want it to be a punch that counts.

I think I've gone on long enough for now and I hope you realize that this is far too brief to really describe all of the attributes and drills you could do, but these are the five essential ingredients for developing true heavy punching power. Be creative, experiment, and develop and pursue the drills or exercises that enhance these 5 attributes and you will get the extra horsepower that increases your punching power. I hope that you find what I've discussed here useful to your training.

In regard to the sum total of everything we've discussed here, the goal of developing the ultimate in punching power is really summed up in this statement. "I want you to be able to hit so hard, that it doesn't matter where you hit your opponent, you will still bring him to his knees.

BONUS ARTICLE 2 of 2

Combatives Is Not an Art

Teaching Combative skills carries with it a certain set of prerequisite strategies and tactics. Combative skills revolves around one word, combat. If I am engaged in combat, I am trying to either incapacitate or kill the enemy. Conversely, that is what he is trying to do to me. That means that if I am teaching or training in Combative skills then these are skills that involve life or death combat. This is where combative skills break from what I would call traditional Martial Arts instruction. Now, knowing that the word martial itself does mean War fighting skills, it is important to see that yes, in the days of its origins, most traditional Martial Arts were based on actual fighting skills. However, over time, almost all of these traditional Arts have become removed from combat and have become highly ritualized, complex methodologies designed more to enhance discipline and physical perfection in practitioners than practical "Real World fighting skills." Now, that is fine if you practice your Martial Art for those reasons. You may say that you study your Martial Arts for arts sake. Fighting is not an art.

The other aspect of martial arts is the sporterized version. This study of martial arts can also be for philosophical and physical perfection. It is expressed through competitions against other practitioners and outcomes can be decided by points given by judges or submissions decided by the fighters. However, there are rules, time limits and referees to stop the contests if injury is likely to either fighter. This is martial sport. Combatives is not a sport.

If you were to go into a traditional karate school you would see karate students fighting against karate attacks. If I were to go into a judo school I would see Judoka defending against Judo attacks. In other words, karate guys train and learn to fight karate guys and judo players learn to fight other judo players.

Not once in my life have I ever had anyone throw a reverse punch at me in a real fight. In martial arts, or martial sports, you get the chance to lose, in real world combatives you cannot lose. You lose – you die. Even as "real" as for example, the UFC is, you do not see a knockout and then the winner execute a rotational neck torque on the unconscious victim to break the neck. This is what would happen if this were a real ultimate fight – to the death. This is the realm of Real World Combative skills.

Combative fighting skills are not passive, they are not philosophical and they are not searching for perfection of technique. You don't need to bow to anybody, you don't need to respect your opponent, there is no sportsmanship and there is nothing that is considered a dirty trick.

In real combat my goal, my only goal, is to impose my will, my physical dominance over the opponent. If I need to hurt, maim, injure or kill him to accomplish that end, I will do so.

Unfortunately most Hand-to-Hand combat training that is available today is an extension of traditional martial arts instruction. There is a logical reason for this. Most instructors in Hand-to-Hand combat got there basic training in traditional martial arts schools. So it only follows that they teach what they were taught.

One of the main differences is that most martial arts are taught from a reactive, or defensive platform. That, in conjunction with the passive philosophy inherent in most traditional (oriental) martial arts is not the strategic basis necessary for use in a life and death environment.

Although combatives training utilizes many of the same skills and techniques that are taught in traditional martial arts systems, there is a major difference, both in teaching philosophy and training, regarding combative skills. True combative training is hard-core, aggressive and brutal both in philosophy, training and application. One of the main differences is that combatives instruction must include, attack or first strike training. This is where the first main break occurs with traditional style systems that are almost solely based on the opponent striking first; i.e., if he punches like this - you counter like that. Since, in reality, most fights are won by the person who strikes first (the surprise attack) then your training must include aggressive, pre-emptive, first strike instruction and practice. This of course, is not taught to the exclusion of reactive, defensive or counter-attacking skills, but it is importantly, a necessary addition. The other fundamental break from traditional teaching is the inclusion of finishing and killing techniques. Now I understand why master Kwon doesn't teach these skills at the neighborhood Tae Kwan Do School, but then again he's not teaching combatives, is he?

Combat skills as generally taught here (in the U.S.) also suffer from the terrible political correctness that is so pervasive in our modern culture. In addition to fear of litigation (I can't teach Johnny how to break someone's neck), most instructors stay way clear of teaching overly aggressive or potentially deadly forms of instruction. However in contrast, combatives as taught to foreign militaries in some cases, is quite different. Soviet Spetsnaz training included trips to morgues and working with dead bodies to practice joint and neck breaking. I also have it on strong intel that in the past, certain units practiced their skills (sometimes lethal) on live prisoners to test their abilities and effectiveness. Remember, the Japanese used to test their swords on live human beings. I'm not saying that these are good practices morally or otherwise. I'm just saying that most of what is taught today, is so watered down that it barely reflects legitimate combat skills. On top of that, it's being taught to individuals that may indeed find themselves engaged in a fight to the death struggle at some point, given our current conflict environment, against our current enemies, (house-to-house, room-to-room fighting). The main difference between martial arts instruction and combative skills training boils down to this. It is the difference between – I'm not going to let this S.O.B. kill me and **I'm going to kill this S.O.B.**

Real world combatives are not complex, impressive or pretty. They are simple, brutal and effective. They rely more on brute strength and naked aggression than perfection of technique and humility.

I had an SAS partner tell me once, "I would have killed him with a sharp stick if I didn't have a rock."

In conclusion, if your combatives program does not include at least some of the ideas that I have just discussed, then perhaps you are just training to learn an art.

-Ernest Emerson

Recommended Reading List for increasing your ability to Detect, Deny and Destroy

Recommended Reading

The Gift of Fear by Gavin De Becker

On Combat by Lt. Col. David Grossman

On Killing by Lt. Col. David Grossman

Defensive Living by Ed Lovette and Dave Spaulding

Under and Alone by William "Billy" Queen

Terror at Beslan by John Giduck

The Mighty Atom by Ed Spielman

Fearless – Adam Brown by Eric Blehm

The Unthinkable By Amanda Ripley

OTHER BOOKS BY ERNEST EMERSON

Chain Reaction Training

Don't buy this book if you are a quitter. It's not for you. You'll hate it, you'll dismiss it, and you won't see any results. If you're a quitter get out of here. Go to the yoga section.

This is a book about hardcore physical training. It's about functional, combat strength and conditioning. It's not about losing weight or bodybuilding. It's about Warrior Strength.

A warrior needs functional strength. A warrior needs Neanderthal strength, Cro-Magnon Strength, the strength that kept our ancestors alive when everything that existed in their world conspired to kill them, and only the strong survived.

A warrior needs the strength that he can use to fight in combat, survive in combat, or save a teammate in combat. In terms of training, that's a whole different creature than a gym membership workout, a bodybuilding workout, or even what most would consider a *hard* training routine.

Think about it like this. What if you need to sprint a quarter-mile over uneven terrain to rescue a teammate out of a downed Helo, sling him over your back and then carry him back a quarter-mile to a safe position. If you run out of gas or God forbid quit, then your buddy dies. You never want to be that guy. If you follow the Chain Reaction Training protocol you won't.

Developed by Black Belt Hall of Famer and renowned tactical instructor Ernest Emerson, the Chain Reaction System is designed to build 100% usable, all-terrain, combat fitness and strength. Drawing on a lifetime of hands-on experience and knowledge, Emerson is interested in one thing only, optimal human performance.

Just like in his combat classes, Emerson is concerned with getting students to perform at their true maximum potential, far beyond what they may think is the limit of their ultimate efforts.

That is what is needed to survive, and prevail in combat. Life-and-death, hand to hand, combat consists of three fundamental components.

1. The skills

2. The mindset

3. Physical strength and conditioning

All three of these have to be optimized in order to engage in combat with the confidence that you will win. And you know, confidence in combat is a huge factor. Without it you are guaranteed to lose.

There's nothing that builds self-confidence to the degree that being strong and fit does. However, few outside of the Special Operations community, Naval Special Warfare (SEALs), or Olympic athletes ever experience the extreme fitness levels that these 1%ers do.

A friend once asked, "Who do you think is the toughest S.O.B. on earth?" The answer? A 135 pound Marine, just out of boot camp. He is the strongest he has ever been. He is in the best condition he's ever been in, and he knows that in a fight, there's no other human being on earth that will run him out of gas. That is confidence.

The Chain Reaction System is a training regimen that will build that extreme level of fitness and, that extreme level of confidence.

Based on a combination of functional strength, and core conditioning exercises, they are pushed to the extreme by completing a chain from start to finish without stopping. It pushes all three components of physical conditioning, the ATP system, the glycolic system, and the aerobic system to new limits. Limits beyond what you once thought you were capable of doing.

Emerson explains in precise, simple, terms how the system works, why the system works, and then gives you a plan for setting up your own regimen, depending on what equipment or facilities you have available. It leaves you with no excuse for not being able to train. In fact, he provides you 25 days of Chain Reaction Routines, his own routines, which amounts to over a month's worth of training. So if you don't get the results promised, it will only be because of your own weak will and lack of resolve. Emerson leaves you with no excuse.

It has been said that the greatest fear of growing old is that other men stop seeing you as being dangerous. The Chain Reaction Training System will keep you very dangerous. Available at: Emersonknives.com

The 7 Strategies of Hand-To-Hand Combat

Black Belt Hall of Famer and Tier One tactical instructor, Ernest Emerson opens the doors to once hidden Strategies, Tactics, and Mentality of the world's deadliest warriors, giving you the tools to upgrade your training in any system, into a truly effective program of combat ready skills.

Emerson's genius is in being able to break down human conflict (combat) into its most basic component parts and then explain them in terms that make perfect sense. Then in turn, he gives you the ability to train and supercharge those components individually so that when they are reassembled the result is an Abrams tank powered by jet engines.

But you must be cautioned, if you're looking for a book on how to block a punch, you won't find it here. This is not a book of techniques. This is about giving you the means to create a supercharged capability to take what you already know to the elite level, ready for actual combat.

The difference between Tier One operators and the rest of us is not that they know more techniques or possess secret skills. They know the same things as we do. They just know how to do them much better. Emerson takes you into his classroom to teach you the real secrets, the forbidden knowledge of the warrior elite, America's Special Operations and Black Ops Units.

The problem with training for real-world hand-to-hand combat skills is that almost all martial arts are over 200 years removed from actual combat and have been softened up or "sporterized" to be palatable to the general public. The difference between conventional training and combatives training is defined by two simple words; intent and intensity. Each needs the other to be maximally effective and conventional martial arts lack both.

Without truly knowing if something will actually work in live combat, how can an instructor teach combat skills to someone whose life may depend on those skills?

If you are ever in a situation where you're face-to-face with pure evil, one who is hell-bent on your destruction, and you're not both physically and mentally prepared for violent, deadly, combat, then that is the day you will likely die.

The author shows that you must be able to bring violence of action against the bad guy to such a degree that it doesn't just counter his attack, but destroys him, for attempting to do you harm.

You will learn how to evaluate your current training against the criteria of the perfect technique, to judge everything you do as to whether it will work in real combat or not, and avoid wasting your valuable time doing things that are of no value.

Learning and applying principles and concepts outlined in this book will give you the confidence you need, to never ever wonder again, "Will this really work, or can I do this?" You will learn that the true mastery of fighting skills is not just based on confidence in the techniques, but ultimately in the confidence you have in yourself.

Some of the subjects covered in detail include;

1. The principles, strategies, and tactics, of combat.

2. The physical, physiological, and psychological effects of combat on the human body and how to use them to your advantage.

3. The Three Laws of Combat and the Six Instinctual Triggers.

4. The high art of preemptive self-defense.

5. The importance of being able to distinguish between capability and capacity.

Combative fighting skills, is not a martial art. It is hard, intense, painful training along with the development of the Warrior Mindset, which is really more valuable than any other skill you possess. Without that mindset and the iron will to win, you are only using half of your power. The other half is in the mind. You will learn how important it is to never neglect one for the other.

Ernest Emerson has worked with members of the Naval Special Warfare Community, Navy SEALs, for over 25 years. He carried a DOD top secret clearance for 15 years. He is the owner of Emerson Knives, Incorporated and the Black Shamrock Combat Academy in Los Angeles California.

Get your copy at:

Emersonknives.com or TheGuardianShepherd.com

7 Essential Skills Needed To Survive A Deadly Attack

In this book, Black Belt Hall of Fame instructor, and Tier One combatives trainer, Ernest Emerson takes you through a detailed dissection of what a human being faces when targeted by dangerous predators in a violent, deadly, assault and what you can do to stop it, dead in its tracks.

Based on the Emerson Combat Systems premise that "Offense *is* Defense," Ernest Emerson explains in detail the Seven Essential Skills you must possess in order to protect not only yourself, but also your loved ones from deadly harm.

In terms everyone can understand the author gives you the same tools, used by Special Operations Operators, CIA Officers and U.S. Navy SEALs, to become a warrior of consummate skills. Skills that go far beyond your physical training in order to train the most powerful weapon you possess, your will. Designed to support any platform of training or skill set that you are currently using, the principles in this book teach you how to take your abilities to that Tier One level of operational functionality. In very simple terms, no matter what you do, this book will give you the tools to do it better.

When you are fighting for your life, you need every possible advantage you can muster. You can't let anything get in the way. The eighth and ninth commandments of "Emerson's Commandments of a Warrior" are as follows:

8. Never do anything without a purpose

9. Never do anything that is useless.

There's no place where these words are more truthful than in hand-to-hand, life-and-death combat.

Each chapter addresses a different aspect of the skills you will need to stack the odds in your favor, should true evil ever come knocking at your door.

Learn the true value of gut feel, and realize that it is your best friend and how you better start listening to what it is telling you.

Never underestimate the power of the will to survive and how it can be harnessed to push you past the tipping point in favor of your survival.

Learn how the, "Loss of Self" is the key to ultimate performance and the ability to fight without fear of harm. That attribute along with the strategies of purpose, means, and intent are all explained in a way that enables you to plug them in to your mindset and training and then express them physically, through your fighting ability. These are the skills and attributes that produce the Warrior Mindset and the Ferocious Resolve that will carry the day on the field of battle.

Emerson continues with a clear discussion of the concept of Moral Clarity. By defining where you stand morally and how far you will go to defend yourself and others, is an all important aspect of self-defense, combatives, and all fighting skills that is seldom if ever, discussed by any other instructors. Emerson forces you to face the cold hard facts of deadly force so you can make an informed decision about your capacities long before you face those realities in the heat of a life-and-death struggle. You cannot be encumbered by hesitation or indecision at a time where fractions of a second can spell the difference between life and death. This book teaches you how to make those decisions before the fact and how those decisions carry the weight that will tip the balance in your favor when push comes to shove.

Get your copy at:

Emersonknives.com or TheGuardianShepherd.com

VIDEOS BY ERNEST EMERSON

Unconventional Edged Weapons Combat I-V

This instructional series is the educational equivalent of a master's degree in Edged Weapons Combat. This is a course. It is a series of instructional evolutions enabling you to super charge your fighting skills. Taught in a progressive layering system using the Accelerated Learning Protocol this course takes you, (regardless of your previous experience or expertise) to a new level of dynamic and unprecedented skill in Edged Weapons Combat. This material has never been available to anyone outside of personal instruction by Ernest Emerson who is regarded as one of the world's leading instructors to military and government agencies worldwide.

VOLUME I
FOUNDATIONS

Building a solid foundation is the fundamental core of developing the Ultimate Fighter. This volume contains the principles and drills needed to develop efficient movement, combat footwork, regaining your stance from the ground and development of the Universal Fighting Stance. Drills and techniques for accessing and deploying your knife are covered, as well as a Bonus Track - Warm up and Stretch.

Get your copy at:

Emersonknives.com or TheGuardianShepherd.com

VOLUME II
TRAINING

This volume, Training teaches you how to develop your skills to their ultimate potential. Covered here are the drills and exercises needed to supercharge your natural, instinctive, abilities. The topics covered include mastering body mechanics, speed training, and developing Ultimate Power. It also includes detailed sections on developing the proper mindset, the universal rules of combat and the anatomy of a knife attack ending with the Golden Rule of Surviving combat.

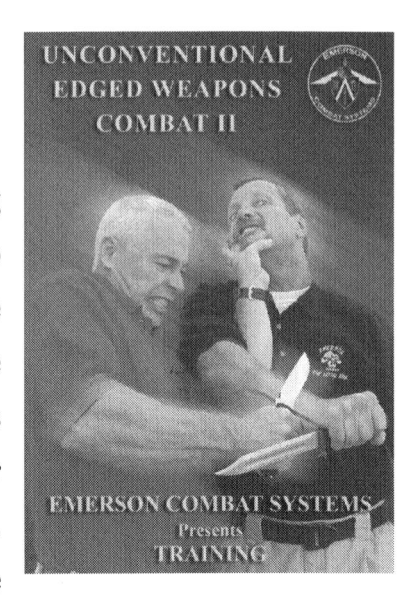

Get your copy at:

Emersonknives.com or TheGuardianShepherd.com

VOLUME III
APPLICATIONS

This is where you learn the tools of the trade. In this third Evolution, Emerson introduces you to all aspects of using the knife as a weapon. Through a series of drills and exercises you will learn how to utilize the principles from foundations and training in actual applications of the knife. Taught here are the strikes, combinations, and techniques including the dynamic art of knife boxing, needed to become a master in the use of a knife and how and when to use them to their maximum potential.

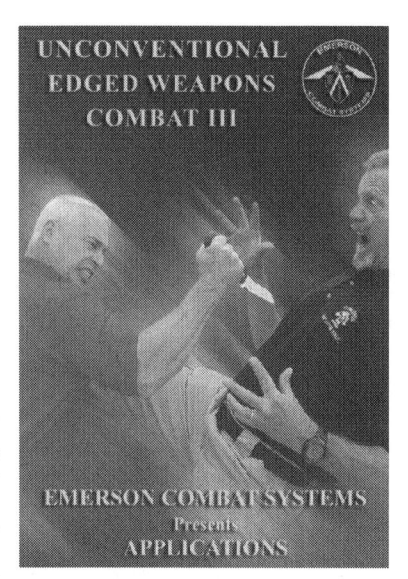

Get your copy at:

Emersonknives.com or TheGuardianShepherd.com

VOLUME IV INTEGRATED WARRIOR

What is the Integrated Warrior Protocol? It is the ability to flow seamlessly between one weapons system and the next. Most arts teach knife techniques, Empty Hand and Grappling as single arts. What happens when you integrate all systems at once? This is the integrated Warrior Protocol. Learn to integrate your knife techniques into your fighting, your boxing, your takedowns and your throws. Learn a system never taught before to the general public and completely revolutionize your fighting ability forever.

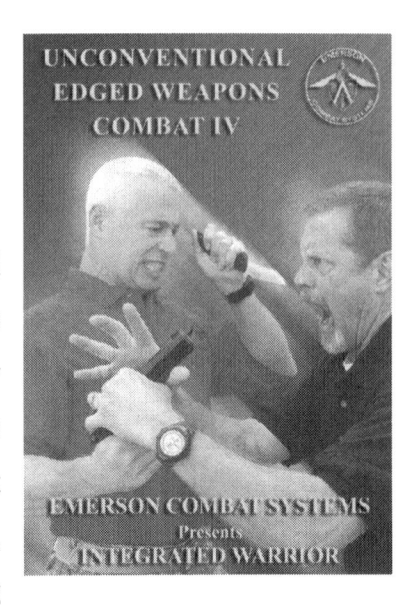

Get your copy at:

Emersonknives.com or TheGuardianShepherd.com

VOLUME V
ADVANCED
TACTICS

Advanced Tactics is where you put everything together. This volume is the culmination of everything taught in Volumes I-IV. Here you will see everything from unarmed techniques against the knife attack, knife against knife, the devastating effectiveness of the "Tiger Gut" and "Buss Saw" and introducing you to the revolutionary and efficient art of knife trapping.

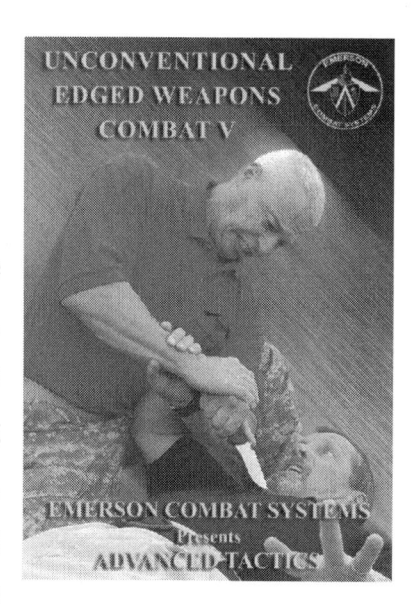

Get your copy at:

Emersonknives.com or TheGuardianShepherd.com

THE COMPLETE COMBAT KARAMBIT

This course introduces you to an entirely new and revolutionary way of fighting with a knife. Developed by Instructor Ernest Emerson to be straightforward, effective, and efficient, this fighting style has to be experienced to be believed. This course is, in large part, the same system that Emerson originated and teaches to elite military units worldwide. This knife fighting style, proven in modern combat, has never been seen by civilian subjects until the release of this course. Modified to exploit the advantages of the Karambit Knife, this amazing fighting system is hard core, bare bones, and brutally effective.

Mr. Emerson teaches a brutal and effective method of fighting that is highly regarded at the highest levels of the U.S. Government and the U.S. Military. Considered a valuable National Asset, Mr. Emerson instructs U.S. Elite Counter - Terrorist Units along with other "Special" Units of the United States Government in the brutal realities of life and death, hand-to-hand Combat.

In this instructional series, The Combat Karambit, you can learn how to use what Mr. Emerson has called one of the best Personal Defense Weapons ever developed - the Karambit Knife. Emerson has taken an age old weapon and thrust it into the 21st century applying his methods of modern, state of the art, combat applications. Now you can learn from the instructor who teaches those considered the Tip of the Spear in America's ongoing war on Terror and are at this moment hunting down and neutralizing those who threaten terror against America.

Get your copy at:

Emersonknives.com or TheGuardianShepherd.com

The Author

Hundreds of books have been published about personal protection, self- defense, conditioning and training, so what makes these so special? Whatever the case, if you are at all like me you are only looking for results. I am a results oriented individual in everything I do and it is driven particularly by how little time I actually have to do anything I want to do. It's the same for you. Without a clear path to results, you'll waste a lot of money and even more valuable, your precious time and in the end walk away disappointed and disillusioned. You'll find that all of these books are designed not so much to teach you something new or to undo what you already know, but instead to enhance the mastery of the skills that you already possess. In essence, to make you more effective, more efficient and to super charge the power that you already have. My goal in everything that I write or teach is to enable that reader or that student to get the absolute most benefit out of their efforts and in the end create an individual who is able to realize the ultimate expression of their performance in these skill sets. Especially if you are ever called to action to use your skills to protect yourself, your loved ones, a teammate, or some other in need of help. It's not so much about what you do, but about being the best at what you do. These books are all written with that goal in mind.

If you go to the web sites – Emerosnknives.com or TheGuardianShepherd.com, you will find access to these and other books by Emerson, along with safety products, self-defense products, the blog, articles, recommendations, videos, and related tips including advice on self-protection and walking the path of a "Warrior Shepherd," one who will willingly and without hesitation stand in harm's way to protect those who are in need.

Mr. Emerson is a noted author lecturer and teacher. He is a respected historian specializing in Roman and Middle Eastern History.

His athletic background includes a college football scholarship, professional baseball. Boxing, kickboxing, Jeet Kune Do, Filipino KALI and Gracie Jiu Jitsu. He has instructed at most of the major combat and shooting schools in the world including Gun Site, The Crucible, International Tactical Training Seminars, Inc., Blackwater, and is a "plank owner" of the think tank, The Combat Research and Development Group. Mr. Emerson was the lead instructor for the company, Global Studies Group International, (GSGI), a training, security and consulting company run by former members of SEAL Team Six, for over 10 years. He is the founder of the Emerson Combat System and has taught his system to "Tier One" military and law enforcement agencies the world over and he is the owner of the Black Shamrock Combat Academy in Los Angeles California.

Known as the "father of the tactical knife" he is also the owner of Emerson Knives, Inc., which produces the most sought after tactical and combat cutlery in the world. Mr. Emerson developed the modern tactical knife and has designed the most recognized iconic knife designs in cutlery history. His work has been featured in scores of articles, magazines, movies and T.V. shows. He is one of the few living artists whose work has been on exhibit at both The New York Metropolitan Museum of Art and The Smithsonian in Washington D.C.

Mr. Emerson can be contacted at:

Ernest@emersonknives.com

Made in the USA
San Bernardino, CA
27 March 2017